"This historic collection of poems by esteemed and budding writers from across the African continent and beyond seeks to confront the ephemerality of life with the permanence of art; it is a testament to the power of poetry to turn grief into art. As WH Auden would have said, these poems start the healing fountains in the deserts of the mourning heart."

—Harry Garuba, Professor and poet, University of Cape Town, South Africa.

"Pius Adesanmi was restless, waging intellectual war against the kind of ignorance that makes oppressed citizens worship their oppressors. *Wreaths for a Wayfarer* is both a poetic tribute, and a remarkable contribution, to that all-important war through beautiful poetry. It is the fight for the enlightenment of all minds that are trapped in caves so they can hear and join the selfless battle for freedom from fiefdoms."

—Obiageli Ezekwesili, 2018 Nobel Prize for Peace nominee and former Vice President of World Bank (Africa Region).

"Fatality has produced its own face of fate in this magisterial anthology, yielding enormous faith in our friend, Pius, as words attack the great loss, lament the unexpected casualty, and expose the revelations of history. Verses speak to our expectations—the daydreaming, the anticipations, even the blessings of a temporary moment. Pius has become a river that will arise from multiple sources to water the earth: a branch will spring from the West, flowing slowly to the East, moving upward to the North, with its Delta marks in the South. A new world is imminent, a new world of rebirth and possibilities, a new world!"

—Toyin Falola, The Jacob and Frances Sanger Mossiker Chair in the Humanities, the University of Texas at Austin

"Richly evocative and engaging, this powerful collection of poems from the heart is a magnificent tribute that emblazons the essence of Pius Adesanmi—joy, love, laughter, wit, brilliance, erudition, nomadism, commitment—whose life was a long poem of peerless beauty; a

melodious song of the breeze and birds of the savannah; an elegant dance to the rhythms of Africa; a resplendent sun that refuses to set.."
—**Obioma Nnaemeka, Chancellor's Professor, Indiana University, Indianapolis, USA, and President, Association of African Women Scholars (AAWS)**.

"*Wreaths for a Wayfarer* is written in divinely eloquent verses—to drums, gongs, flutes and songs—by citizens of the world of words, in whose hearts the 'wayfarer' lives. It is an assemblage of kindred tongues creating and recreating a new future from an unrelieved past and a censured present, around the archetypal wayfarer. This collection . . . is a rare accomplishment. I doubt if this can be surpassed. I may have seen (but cannot recall) a single volume thrust upon my hapless laps with such a climate of paradoxes—a synthetic Mass of threnody, elegy, requiems and hope, rebirth and redemption around a single living-dead: Pius Adebola Adesanmi. *Igi dagbara j'eno otin* (A lone log that brews a pot of corn wine to intoxicating ferment...)"
—*Olu Obafemi,* **Professor of English and Dramatic Literature, Fellow of the Nigerian Academy of Letters (FNAL), and recipient of the Nigeria National Order of Merit (NNOM).**

"The wayfarers and exiles, so admirably represented by Pius Adesanmi and others in this anthology, prove a zealous identification with the native land, from far and near. They left but never forgot. They have had an open readiness to acquire new knowledge and to purge moribund ones in pursuit of life-affirming directions. This, indeed, is the gravamen of this anthology: that the death of one exemplar. . . has yielded a reason to intensify a resistant ethic to the devastation and dilapidation that have become sources of trauma and regrets across country and continent."
—**Odia Ofeimun, Poet and former President of the Association of Nigerian Authors (ANA)**

What tales shall the wayfarer tell
When time and tide
And the pool of ancestral blood
Return him to his native land?
— Pius Adesanmi, "The Wayfarer"

If I take the wings of the morning and dwell
in the uttermost parts of the sea,
even there your hand shall lead me,
and your right hand shall hold me
— Psalm 139: 9-10

in the beginning was the Voice
and the Voice was with Thunder
and the Thunder roared with lightning
and broke into a reign of rains.
—Nduka Otiono, "Rainsong"

Wreaths for a Wayfarer

Wreaths for a Wayfarer
An Anthology of Poems in Honour of Pius Adesanmi

Edited by

NDUKA OTIONO
&
UCHECHUKWU UMEZURIKE

Daraja Press

Published by Daraja Press
https://darajapress.com
PO Box 99900 BM 735 664,
RPO Ottawa South, Ottawa, ON, K1S 5G2, Canada

© 2020 Nduka Otiono & Uchechukwu Umezurike
All rights reserved

ISBN 9781988832333 (softcover)
ISBN 9781988832340 (ebook)

Library and Archives Canada Cataloguing in Publication

Title: Wreaths for a wayfarer : an anthology of poems in honour of Pius Adesanmi / edited by Nduka
  Otiono & Uchechukwu Umezurike.
Names: Otiono, Nduka, 1964- editor. | Umezurike, Uche Peter, 1975- editor.
Identifiers: Canadiana (print) 20190132949 | Canadiana (ebook) 20190132981 | ISBN 9781988832333
   (softcover) | ISBN 9781988832340 (ebook)
Subjects: LCSH: African poetry (English)—21st century.
Classification: LCC PR9346 .W74 2019 | DDC 821.008/0896—dc23

Dedication

*To Pius Adesanmi, wayfarer who sang the psalm
and boarded the iron bird that lost its bearing
and nose-dived onto the earth.*

*And to all other African writers
Whose life's flights were prematurely
felled by death*

. . . Continue to rest in power with the ancestors.

Contents

Acknowledgements	xxiii
Foreword Odia Ofeimun	xxv
Introduction: Death and an African Digital Towncrier Nduka Otiono	1
Introit: Coffin in the sky Niyi Osundare	16

Part I. WAYFARER

Scabha or The Sliding Door Operator Sihle Ntuli	21
When an Iroko Falls Iquo Diana Abasi	25
How to Survive War in Nigeria Iquo Diana Abasi	27
I Wet the Earth, I Sing You Wreaths... Fareed Agyakwah	29
Harvest IV Funmi Aluko	31
Wayfarer Funmi Aluko	33
The Wayfarer Saudat Salawudeen	34
End of Forever Saudat Salawudeen	35

Muse of Homecoming	36
Justus K. S. Makokha	
Encore	38
Agatha Agema	
Now that I know young birds die in flight	40
Segun Michael Olabode	
The Water-Pot is Broken	42
Susan Bukky Badeji	
from absence, memory and farther	44
Obemata	
Umbilicals	46
Tijah Bolton-Akpan	
The Pilgrim Unbound	47
Clara Ijeoma Osuji	
Eclipsed at Noon	50
Abdulaziz Abdulaziz	
To the Daughters	51
Abdulaziz Abdulaziz	
The Traveler	52
Abiodun Bello	
For the Wayfarer	54
Chifwanti Zulu	
The Acts of Brother Pius	55
'Bunmi Ogungbe	
Backing His Daughter: For Pius, on Facebook	57
Jane Bryce	
Avoiding Sunlight	58
Unoma Azuah	
Akásọlérí (Mourners)	59
Kọ́lá Túbọ̀sún	
Last Tweets	61
Kọ́lá Túbọ̀sún	

Farewell, Wayfarer	63
Oyinkansade Fabikun	
Solitaire	65
Kafilat Oloyede	
How to Keep the Wake for a Shooting Star	66
Chuma Nwokolo	
Eagle	67
Uzo Odonwodo	
In Memoriam	69
Uzo Odonwodo	
Can You Do This Thing?	70
Sarah Katz-Lavigne	
Lights	72
John Chizoba Vincent	
The Meteorite	74
Omowumi Olabode Steven Ekundayo	
Black Box	75
Ian Keteku	
Paramour of the Pen	77
Abraham Tor	
Flying Coffin	78
James Onyebụchi Nnaji	
Looking for the Dead	79
James Onyebụchi Nnaji	
The Eagle Perched	80
Moses Ogunleye	
A Pius Flight	81
Kennedy Emetulu	
Kwanza for Pius	82
Ifesinachi Nwadike	
Dream-mare	83
Nidhal Chami	

A Walk in the Graveyard — 85
  Chimeziri C. Ogbedeto
Payo — 86
  Biko Agozino
Iku — 87
  Peter Olamakinde Olapegba
He left — 88
  Amatoritsero Ede
Spousal Loss — 89
  Peter Olamakinde Olapegba
The Face of My Savior is the Ordinary Moment — 90
  Gloria Nwizu
Denouement — 92
  Gloria Nwizu
A Conversation between Two Young Cousins — 93
  Ethel Ngozi Okeke
Sunday Flight — 95
  Emman Usman Shehu
Departure — 97
  Ivor Agyeman-Duah
The Count — 99
  Uthpala Dishani Senaratne
Rude Shock — 100
  Olajide Salawu
Saturday 12:56 — 101
  Ludwidzi M. K. Mainza
Daughter — 102
  Ludwidzi M. K. Mainza
Tough Love — 103
  Nnorom Azuonye
In the Midst of it All, I am... — 104
  Anushya Ramakrishna

Haiku – Ai-Ku (Immortality)	106
Adesanya Adewale Adeshina	
He Rose	107
Adesanya Adewale Adeshina	
A Singing Bird	108
Adesanya Adewale Adeshina	
Arrivant	109
Akua Lezli Hope	
EarthWork Sestina	112
Akua Lezli Hope	
Animalia, Chordata, Mammalia, Proboscidea	114
Akua Lezli Hope	
Poem of Relief: When Your Sadness is Alive	116
Kennedy Hussein Aliu	
If I Seek	117
Kennedy Hussein Aliu	
When You Ask me About my Teacher	119
Kennedy Hussein Aliu and Leyda Jocelyn Estrada Arellano	
The Eagle is not the Quills and Talons	121
Olumide Olaniyan	
without a farewell	122
Nduka Otiono	
After the Funeral	124
Nduka Otiono	
Fugitives from the Violence of Truth	125
Efe Paul-Azino	
Just but a Journey	127
Sam Dennis Otieno	

Part II. REQUIEMS

Elegy for Pius	131
Helon Habila	
This Exodus Has Birthed a Song	132
Echezonachukwu Nduka	
where to find you: a requiem	133
Echezonachukwu Nduka	
Blown	134
Richard Inya	
words melt in his mouth	135
Peter Midgley	
Requiem for the Fallen / Mogaka o ole	137
Lebogang Disele	
To Our Hero: Rest in Peace	140
Lebogang Disele	
What Shall We Do to Death?	141
Winlade Israel	
A Star Just Fell	142
Winlade Israel	
Requiem	143
Peter Akinlabi	
Requiem for Pius	144
Rasaq Malik Gbolahan	
Wayfarer	145
Rasaq Malik Gbolahan	
Twirling the Beads of Grief...	146
Tade Aina	
Say me Rebellion	147
Kingsley L. Madueke	
When this Calabash Breaks	149
Kingsley L. Madueke	

Requiem for the Wayfarer	151
Adesina Ajala	
Song of Sorrow	152
Soji Cole	
Planting Season	153
Anote Ajeluorou	
For Our Departed Bard	155
Maria Ajima	
Memory of Tear	157
Joshua Agbo	
Why?	158
Margaret Wairimu Waweru	
Letter to Dad	160
Margaret Wairimu Waweru	
Missing Voices	162
Ugochukwu P. Nwafor	
Tears on Canvas	164
Wesley Macheso	
Nausea	165
Wesley Macheso	
This Easter	166
Wesley Macheso	
When I Am Gone	167
Maryam Ali Ali	
Nothing Has Changed	168
Maryam Ali Ali	
Protest	169
Ejiofor Ugwu	
Our Voice is Gone	171
Janet James Ibukun	
Agadaga Iroko / Giant Iroko	173
Sunny Iyke U. Okeigwe	

This Poetry	175
James Tar Tsaaior	
The Passing of Pius	179
Uzor Maxim Uzoatu	
Light Dims to Shine Forever	180
Akachi Adimora-Ezeigbo	
You Bled Africa!	182
Mitterand Okorie	
To the Muse of Isanlu: A Salute	184
'BioDun J. Ogundayo	
you remain with us	186
Nkateko Masinga	
A Bit of Narcissism	188
Okwudili Nebeolisa	
Bereavement	189
Okwudili Nebeolisa	
Dirge for the Departed	191
Koye-Ladele Mofehintoluwa	
If Only	192
Femi Abidogun	
Falling Birds	193
Yusuff Abdulbasit	
Immortality	194
Yusuff Abdulbasit	
Harvest of Deaths	195
Yemi Atanda	
The Horse and the Tortoise	197
Yemi Atanda	
The Chorus Is Death	199
Ubaka Ogbogu	
Breaking Bread	201
Obiwu	

Still They Hunt for Emmett Till   202
   Obiwu
on wisdom's wings   203
   Jumoke Verissimo

Part III. HOMECOMING

The Indent (For Pius)   207
   Uche Nduka
when the sun sets   209
   Adejumo Uthman Ajibola
Aridunun Akowe   211
   Dahunsi Ayobami
Pius: Myth, Mystic, Mystery   213
   Tenibegi Karounwi
Returning the Light as Wreath   217
   Ndubuisi Martins (Aniemeka)
Naija is a Badly-Behaved Poem   218
   Ndubuisi Martins (Aniemeka)
Confessions of a Gypsy   219
   Richard Kayode O. James
When the Pious Die   220
   Uchenna-Franklin Ekweremadu
Song of the Pilgrim   221
   Obinna Chukwudi Ibezim
Pius, the Seed   222
   Celina O. Aju-Ameh
Cloud Coffin   223
   Tola Ijalusi
Letter to My Father   224
   Ololade Akinlabi Ige
I Journey Quietly Home   225
   Martin Ijir

Hopeful People	226
Ndaba Siban	
Explaining My Depression to You	227
Yusuf Taslemat Taiwo	
The Broken Quill	229
Nathanael Tanko Noah	
we do not know how to carry this pain	231
Edaki Timothy. O	
Stars, Out	232
S. Su'eddie Vershima Agema	
Converging Skies and Shadows	233
S. Su'eddie Vershima Agema	
Will You?	235
Biodun Bamgboye	
Farewell	236
Maryam Gatawa	
Transit to Kenya	238
Anthony Enyone Ohiemi	
Abiku Agba	239
Usman Oladipo Akanbi	
Evening Bird	240
Bayowa Ayomide Micheal	
Withered Green	241
Augustine Ogechukwu Nwulia	
Home Call…047	243
Onuchi Mark Onoruoiza	
Outshining the Stars	244
Onuchi Mark Onoruoiza	
The Eagle Has Fallen	245
Manasseh Gowk	
Farewell	246
Manasseh Gowk	

Death   247
     Khalid Imam

The Flood   248
     Khalid Imam

Blue Skies   249
     Yejide Kilanko

This Very Goodbye   250
     Nseabasi S. J. King

The Deserted Road or Elegy for Pius Adesanmi   251
     Daniel Olaoluwa Whyte

What My Father Said on His Death Bed   252
     Gbenga Adesina

Wayfarer   253
     James Yeku

One Meets Two   255
     James Yeku

First Goodbye   256
     D.M. Aderibigbe

Monster   257
     Afam Akeh

where you are now   258
     Raphael d'Abdon

When the Curtains Fall   260
     Uchechukwu Umezurike

Part IV. A Selection from Pius Adesanmi's "The Wayfarer and Other Poems"

"The Wayfarer"   263
     Pius Adesanmi

Ah, Prometheus!   265
     Pius Adesanmi

Odia Ofeimun: The Brooms Take Flight	266
Pius Adesanmi	
To the Unfathomable One	268
Pius Adesanmi	
Message from Aso Rock to a Poet in Exile	269
Pius Adesanmi	
Entries	270
Pius Adesanmi	

Part V. POSTLUDE

A Prose-Poem, a Tribute, and a Wreath for Pius Adesanmi	275
Anu'a-Gheyle Solomon Azoh-Mbi	
When and If...	278
Pamela J. Olúbùnmi Smith	
Contributors	279
About the editors	300

Acknowledgements

We are grateful to everyone who submitted poems for consideration for publication in this book. In all, we received submissions from 267 writers, comprising established and budding poets across the world. Without their submissions this book would not have sprouted. Regrettably, we could not plant all the seeds submitted to us in this volume. Still, we would like to thank both those whose poems appear in this volume as well as those whose poems, for various reasons, did not fit into the book. Indeed, as I had written in one poem—"Moon Dance (Listen Sylvia)" — "beauty is in the eyes of the editor/ the editor's indecision is final."

We would like to thank all those who supported this project from inception to completion. From a list too long to recount here, we would like to thank Mrs. Muyiwa Adesanmi, Pius's widow, who sanctioned the project and granted us permission to republish a selection from Pius's sole collection of poems, *The Wayfarer and Other Poems*; Promise Okekwe of Oracle Books, Pius's publisher, for the vision to originally publish that collection and for permission to republish some of the poems; our publishers—Firoze Manji of Daraja Press, Canada, and Eghosa Imasuen and Anwuli Ojogwu of Narrative Landscape Press, Nigeria—for their confidence in this anthology; Professor Blair Rutherford, for his enthusiasm which watered the roots of the project; Kika Otiono, Emma Bider and Sarah George for editorial assistance.

We are indebted to Ochi Ogbuaku and Moses Ogunleye, for conceptual suggestions for the cover; and even more indebted to Victor Ehikamenor, for the brilliant cover designs that beautify the book.

We thank Odia Ofeimun for writing the poignant Foreword to this anthology. In the same vein, we appreciate the endorsements received from Obioma Nnaemeka, Oby Ezekwesili, Harry Garuba, Toyin Falola, Odia Ofeimun, and Olu Obafemi.

We would like to thank colleagues at the Institute of African Studies, Carleton University—Christine Duff, June Payne and Femi Ajidahun—for solidarity. We also extend our appreciation to colleagues at the University of Alberta—Lahoucine Ouzgane, Albert Braz, and

Michael Litwack—for their support while Uche, their student, worked on this project.

Finally, without the love and understanding of our respective families—the Otionos of Ottawa and the Umezurikes of Edmonton—the sacrifice that sustained putting this book together within a short gestation period may not have been possible. To family, we say: One love!

Foreword

ODIA OFEIMUN

Pius Adesanmi was 'my personal person', as he was to so many people across the globe. To say it in pidgin English is to testify to his peculiar Nigerian mystique: a hearty sense of fellow-feeling, concern and caring; purposive and stubborn, daring and self-sacrificing; full of celebrative embroilment in the hard issues of contemporary struggles for a better and more humane society in Nigeria, Africa and the world. A poet and radical professor of Comparative and post-colonial Literature at Carlton University in Canada, a public intellectual and spokesperson for a variety of good causes, and a man whose intellectual fire power was the toast of a generation! It explains why he quickly became the poster personage of the 157 passengers, all victims, aboard Ethiopian Airline 737 which crashed en-route to Nairobi on 10th March 2019.

Only a year before, preternaturally accident prone, Pius had survived yet another horrid motor accident during a visit to Nigeria that left him after time in hospital and therapy with a bad limp. Now, his death was having an intercontinental fare, a widening loop of grief from campus to campus, city to city across Nigeria, Canada, Europe and America, across Africa's many diasporas, and spooling a comity of mourners and sympathizers all keyed into a worldwide eruption on the social media. In the annals of the travelling world, few outreaches, after a crash, ever galvanized as much fellowship and outpouring of fellow feeling—a literal barnstorming of emotional identification with the dead. The scandal of a computer glitch as the source of the tragedy added a deep and inscrutable post-modern sourness to the picture.

It would have been too much a yawn of self-forgetting if, after the worldwide demonstration of shock, grief and anger at the death of the poet/scholar and public intellectual, there was no scribal acknowledgement, such as this anthology, to commemorate it. In Nigerian literature, such a yawn, voluntary or involuntary, would have been out of sync with custom. It happens that quite a tradition of communality bobs up among Nigerian poets whenever a tragic bind takes away a fellow poet. To register it: the first such anthology in English followed the death of Christopher Okigbo, Nigeria's most celebrated poet, at the age of 35, fighting on the Biafran side during the Nigerian civil war of 1967-70. The anthology was edited by Chinua Achebe and Dubem Okafor with the title *Don't Let Him Die*. It signified the awe of death and its waste of youth and creative energy. *Don't let him die* set the template for a generation that witnessed so much death and dying but was always seeking through memory and dream to transpose mourning sequences into a defence and prolongation of life.

Along came the judicial murder of Ken Saro-Wiwa, poet and dramatist, a past President of the Association of Nigerian Authors and leader of the Movement for the Survival of Ogoni People (MOSOP)! It offered occasion for a corpus titled *For Ken, For Nigeria*, edited by Nduka Otiono and Epaphras Osondu during what is generally referred to as Nigeria's "locust days". It absorbed the grisly circumstance of the military dictatorship of dark-goggled General Sani Abacha, who hanged Ken and his eight Ogoni kinsmen, stirring up world-wide denunciation and, in the domestic space, defiance along the tradition of not letting the poet die. In an environment in which the assertion and maintenance of the human spirit is in ever short supply, letting the poet die, as when his and her words cannot be accessed or echoed by other poets, is to risk letting down our sense of the human, especially in the use of language and its posit of fellow-feeling across time.

Therefore, it is true to form and tradition, that this anthology, *Wreaths for A Wayfarer: An Anthology in honour of Pius Adesanmi*, brings together an informal fellowship of poets, from across the world, to commemorate the death of one of its own, in a rite of poetic affirmation at once a projection of and defence of the memory of one individual whose life and death touched fellow human beings across nations and continents. In choosing the title, the editors, Nduka Otiono and Uchechukwu Umezurike, and the contributors to this anthology, have displayed creative enterprise by tapping into the poetic instincts of *The Wayfarer and Other Poems*, Pius Adesanmi's lone collection of poems before his demise. Offerings from the collection form a strategic part, a fourth dimension, no less, after the tripartite division of this anthology into wayfarers, requiems and homecoming. Conjointly, they provide autobiographical and engagingly biographical excursus and a historical sanction for the many insights dredged out of imaginative accommodation of the Adesanmi mystique.

Decidedly, the theme of wayfaring as the riveting core of this anthology outpoints the call of mourning and grief. It takes a cue from Pius Adesanmi's personal mythology as an abiku, dying and being reborn, in a persistent recourse to reincarnation; until overtaken by a holding operation in the form of countermanding rites that blunted his zeal for a return journey to the other world. It can be imagined that the rites kept him an impassioned denizen of trans-border transactions, from other worlds, across English and French Africa, in spatial and cultural-linguistic terms, and relocating from Nigeria to Canada from whence he commuted with the rest of the world in a fairly intense over-drive! At least, for a while. Pius signposted his status as a wayfarer by insisting on the need to right whatever wrongs there were and celebrating extant possibilities before moving on to the next port. In the final analysis, as depicted by many avid contributions from far and wide in this anthology, his death was simply the ultimate consummation of that personal mythology of an abiku relocating from the known world through a connecting flight to Nairobi.

But there is a more scatological sense in which his status as a wayfarer comes into the picture: he happened to be a member of that age-set, sadly turning into a generation, that had to migrate from what Frantz Fanon once called the 'geography of hunger', an immiserated Africa as part of that Third World hegemonized over by former colonizers; an Africa in which the brightest and the best suffered the shabby mono-parties of flag independence and the mis-governments of corrupt and egregious militariats expelling a lot of talent and freewill into exile. And doing so by whatever stratagems they could muster! This is the sore point in the verses from *The Wayfarer* excerpted for this anthology. Deploying the habits of inter-text and dialogue so common among Nigerian poets, the story is of the post-independence age-set to which he belonged, an age-set that one of his poems ("Odia Ofeimun: The Brooms Take Flight") charges me with seeking out for special civic duties. I admit to being passionate, very passionate, even now, about that age-set or age-grade; and 'criss-crossing deltas and savannahs/in search of tender palmfronds/.... found in abundance/in Ibadan, Lagos and Nsukka", and beyond, to turn into a nation-saving laager. His death, sadly, has removed a most vibrant plinth off that age grade.

Indeed, Pius was a plinth of idealism personified. To protect and project a much-abused country and continent away from the many plagues bedevilling our history, he enjoyed intellectual sparring, arguments, even sheer roforofo fights on the pages of newspapers and magazines. As he writes in his poem, "Odia Ofeimun: The Broom Takes Flight", "we need new brooms/to clear the rot/and renew our lot". He was playing the "round leather" (or soccer ball) forward when he wrote the other part of the corpus of poems, "To the Unfathomable One", (after a telephone conversation with Nduka Otiono), one of the editors of this anthology! It was typical Pius Adesanmi saying: "Listen more to the brother from Ikere Ekiti/For man can only mean to man/Brother to brother/in the absence of darkness/". He was bidding for strong commitments; at the risk of altercations between fellow wayfarers. In a country where "120 million corpses pretend to live" and those who tried to dream had to confront "generals …. allergic to dreams", he spoke from a high sense of moral compulsion, not a mere need for escape that included a choice of exile. Expatriation? the pleasures and anxieties of it? Nothing could exhaust the tougher motivation that the novelist and poet, Helon Habila puts so pointedly, in "Elegy For Pius": the plan was:

> We would win accolades, break records, storm citadels
> And bring home the laurels—
> We would return in time to stitch the broken fabric of our land
>
> But [it was] … not how we planned it, to become homeless in this world
> Visitors on the streets of Lagos, eternally departing and returning

Habila's lines emerge from the teeth of an awareness that the 'departing and returning' of the wayfarers, those who opted for exile, did not take away the predisposition to defy the bad habits that continue to plague the homeland. As the poem insists, "Defiant we glow" in pro-bono performances across a motley of issues and causes. The wayfarers and exiles, so admirably represented by Pius Adesanmi and others in this anthology, prove a zealous identification with the nativeland, from far and near. They left but never forgot. They have had an open readiness to acquire new knowledge and to purge moribund ones in pursuit of life-affirming directions. This, indeed, is the gravamen of this anthology: that the death of one exemplar with so much personal integrity and commitment to disburse, has yielded a reason to intensify a resistant ethic to the devastations and dilapidations that have become sources of trauma and regrets across country and continent.

Overall, the poems in this anthology are coincident in their empathies with The Introit, titled "Coffin In The Sky", by Nigerian poet Niyi Osundare, declaiming "we are too tired/ of burying our best". Echezonachukwu Nduka reminds us that "we turn to pathways now clear because you, wayfarer /dared to walk ahead". It is a good reason, as the South African poet, Nkateko Masinga writes "never to speak in the past tense" about our honoured dead because naming them "in the universe of was/ belies the fact:" that they remain with us. Specific to Pius Adesanmi: *Wreaths for A Wayfarer* adds up to why, after *You are not A Country, Africa* and *Naija No Dey Carry Last*, he would always remain with us.

Introduction: Death and an African Digital Towncrier

NDUKA OTIONO

> *She is the Gaelic muse, for she gives inspiration to those she persecutes. The Gaelic poets die young, for she is restless, and will not let them remain long on earth—this malignant phantom.*
> —William Butler Yeats, "Fairy and Folk Tales of the Irish Peasantry." (81)

> *It is not enough . . . to repeat the empty affirmation that the author has disappeared . . . Instead, we must locate the space left empty by the author's disappearance, follow the distribution of gaps and breaches, and watch for the openings this disappearance uncovers.*
> —Michel Foucault, "What is an Author?" (209)

It is hard, even for the most gifted psychic, to accurately predict how they would react to the passing of someone dear to them either physically or virtually—especially in the social media age where imaginary friendships appear concrete. And so, when Pius Adebola Adesanmi (aka Payo), the popular Nigerian-Canadian public intellectual and professor of English and director of the Institute of African Studies at Carleton University, Ottawa, Canada, turned out to be one of the 159 casualties of the March 10, 2019 Ethiopian Airlines Flight 302 crash in Bishoftu shortly after take-off from Addis Ababa international airport, his tragic demise evoked unpredictable reactions. It was a Sunday morning, typically an uneventful time of the week when people generally float between nursing hangovers from Saturday night indulgences, religious rituals, reflections on the passing week and a slow embrace of a new week. In the swollen moments of that morning, news of the doomed flight crashed through the old analogue radio in my study. But the mind, unacquainted with the dimensions of such news, would not imagine familiarity with a victim. As tragic as a commercial plane crash may be, with hundreds of people often being killed, the possibility of one knowing a victim seemed remote.[1] I had spent time with Adesanmi in the office a day before he travelled. I could not envisage that he was one of the passengers in the crash two days after our last meeting. As the rumour spread that Pius might have been a passenger on that flight, I simply could not connect with it, even though I knew he would be on his way to Kenya via Addis Ababa that weekend. In my confusion, I argued with my wife, Onyi, that the flight that crashed must have been one flying the opposite direction—from Nairobi to Addis Ababa. It took news coming from official and social media sources for reality to finally set in.

Adesanmi was popular amongst Nigeria's netizens. With his premature death, the global reputation of the public intellectual increased exponentially. He was one of 18 Canadians and citizens of about 35 other countries on board that flight. The plane crash sparked one of the most troubling developments in aviation history, the reverberations of which are still being felt around the world. It shook the very foundations of the most recognizable aircraft manufacturers, Boeing. The nature of the crash has refocused global attention to aircraft safety and the sharp profit-driven practices of some global corporations. In fact, some critics have gone to the extent of insinuating

---

1. The statistics paint a more detailed picture. According to specialist report citing US Federal Aviation Authority (FAA), "[t]he number of flights performed globally by the airline industry has been steadily increasing since the early 2000's and is expected to reach 39.4 million in 2019," an increase of more than one million from the 38.1 million recorded for 2018. For the United States alone, to say nothing about flights across the world, "every day, the FAA's Air Traffic Organization (ATO) provides service to more than 42,000 flights and 2.5 million airline passengers across more than 29 million square miles of airspace... At any given moment there are more than 5,000 aircraft traversing the U.S. skies" (Mazareanu, *Statista*, n.p.). Yet, within a 74-year window (1945 to 2019), the United States of America holds the record for the country with the highest number of fatal civil airliner accidents: 854. However, it should be pointed out that based on analysis of details available on *aviation-safety.net* database, most of the accidents were non multi-passenger flights.

that corporate greed played an underhand role in the circumstances that led to the crashing of the Ethiopian Airline flight and the Lion Air flight in Indonesia just six months before.[2]

Against the background of my quarter-of-a-century relationship with Adesanmi as a friend, co-traveller on many social and professional planes, as well as a colleague at Carleton's Institute of African Studies (IAS), it seemed inevitable that I would play key roles in marking his final rite of passage, especially as our shared African cultural heritage required an understanding of life as a celebration defined by ceremonies. I thought that an anthology of creative writing would be an appropriate way to immortalize him and his legacy. Uchechukwu Umezurike, with whom I chose to work on this anthology, reminded me of the book *Don't Let Him Die*, an anthology in honour of the great Nigerian poet Christopher Okigbo co-edited by Chinua Achebe and Dubem Okafor. He also reminded me of one other African poet who also died in a plane crash on August 29, 1960—the Senegalese Negritude poet, David Diop. The remembrances further galvanized work on this anthology in honour of Pius Adesanmi, albeit while being mindful of the cautionary observation of the pioneer critics of African literature Gerald Moore and Ulli Beier that "anthologies based on a sense of duty rather than of pleasure are always unreadable" (28).

We decided to call the anthology *Wreaths of a Wayfarer*, inspired by the idea of laying symbolic wreaths at the funeral of the author of *The Wayfarer and Other Poems*. The spontaneity and finality with which the title of the anthology *Wreaths of a Wayfarer* came to me easily contextualizes the circumstances that produced the anthology. With the uncertainty about the possibility of a funeral at the time—the remains were later recovered and interred at a cemetery in Ottawa on October 26, 2019—laying virtual poetic wreaths for the author of *The Wayfarer and Other Poems* appeared to me as a natural sequence. That is, in lieu of the formal and traditional consecration of the body

---

2. See for example, Lori Aratani's report, "New lawsuit alleges that Boeing put profit over people with 737 Max," *Washington Post*, April 8, 2019. https://www.washingtonpost.com/local/trafficandcommuting/new-lawsuit-alleges-that-boeing-put-profit-over-people-with-737-max/2019/04/08/d93a7eba-5a36-11e9-a00e-050dc7b82693_story.html

to Mother Earth. *Wreaths of a Wayfarer* is, therefore, the collective "wreaths" laid by a dispersed community of writers unsettled by the untimely loss of Adesanmi. These poetic wreaths are not only for Pius Adesanmi, but also in honour of the other victims of the disaster that included a nine-month-old baby; a Kenyan man who lost his wife, daughter and three grandchildren; a Canadian family comprising three generations—Kosha Vaidya and her husband, Prerit Dixit, travelling with their two teenage daughters, Ashka and Anushka, and with Kosha's parents, Pannagesh and Hansini (BBC News).[3] Seen this way, the archetypal image of the wayfarer in the title of this anthology captures the enormity and breadth of the losses. Beyond the focus on Adesanmi, the anthology represents, on a wider lens, a tribute to all those everyday people engaged in quotidian transnational movements that rule our lives in an era of rapid globalization.

Whoever has stared death in the face would understand the significance of the tragic manner of Adesanmi's disappearance from this physical realm in the sense expressed in the epigraph from Michel Foucault above. Death had courted him a few times. First, as an *abiku* child about which he so eloquently writes in his poem, "Entries"[4] and which I discuss in detail below. Then, just one year before the plane crash, Adesanmi was involved in a car accident in Nigeria during the summer of 2018 when I too was in Nigeria. He had sent me the photos of the accident and of his injuries which I have not summoned up the courage to look at again. Although one can think of death as the "omnipresent halo" above our heads as I write in my poem "Swansong" (290), anyone who has suffered a near-death experience and defied the close shave, as I have, will understand the difficulty of writing at that moment. I have had to do so twice—first when I was stabbed in the back and was inspired by the incident to write "The Night Hides with a Knife"; and second when I was shot at point-blank range in Apapa, Lagos, in December 2001 and have not quite been able to exorcise the trauma in writing. And now Pius's death formed another "omnipresent halo" above our heads.

---

3. See *BBC News*, "Ethiopian Airlines: The Victims of a Global Tragedy." https://www.bbc.com/news/world-africa-47522028, April 4, 2019.
4. See the poem in Part IV of this anthology.

Some believe that Pius foretold his end: just before he boarded his plane, he posted Psalm 139: 9–10[5] on his Facebook Timeline. In addition, he had written his epitaph which he wished would be posted on his grave: "Here lies Pius Adesanmi who tried as much as he could to put his talent in the service of humanity and flew away home one bright morning when his work was over."[6] Prophetic or not, it seems more than coincidental that Adesanmi entitled his first and only book of poetry *The Wayfarer and Other Poems*. For he was, indeed, a wayfarer. Here was a 47-year young, high-flying father of two adorable daughters—Damilare, 12, and Tise, 7—cruising at the peak of his career, but felled by a high-tech iron bird that could not remain in the skies to bear him and the other passengers to their destination. Adesanmi had successfully completed the longer stretch of his journey across the Atlantic from the Diaspora where he lived, only to succumb to a catastrophic crash six minutes into the shorter connection to his destination in Mother Africa. Prior to the trip, he had lamented that he would be spending four days travelling on the one-week assignment—two days going from and two days returning to Canada. Before his departure he completed arrangements for two major events towards the end of the winter semester of the academic year (2019): a) a dinner party on March 15th in honor of IAS guest speaker, Nafisa Essop of the University of Johannesburg (also a visiting professor at Cornell then); b) the IAS annual general meeting and graduate students annual symposium scheduled for April 11th.

---

5. "If I rise on the wings of the dawn, / if I settle on the far side of the sea,/ even there your hand will guide me,/ your right hand will hold me fast." Also see Jamilah Nasir's "OBITUARY: In our hearts lies Pius Adesanmi, the prophet who foretold his death" published in *The Cable* Online newspaper, March 12, 2019. https://www.thecable.ng/obituary-in-our-hearts-lie-pius-adesanmi-the-prophet-who-foretold-his-death
6. The Nigerian writer Chuma Nwokolo offers more information about this epitaph in his tribute to Adesanmi. He recalls that: "Back in 2013, in the African Writing interview I referenced earlier, I had asked forty-one writers to draft epitaphs for their future tombstones. Professor Adesanmi sent me his answer in a Facebook message at 3am on 21st August 2013". For details see Nwokolo's "An Epitaph for Pius Adesanmi," https://nwokolo.com/y/an-epitaph-for-pius-adesanmi/

Adesanmi's vivacious personality and writings were evident even in his semi-formal communication. As Director of Carleton's Institute of African Studies, he called his periodic updates on the milestones of faculty, staff and students affiliated to IAS "Rooftop News" or "Dispatches from the Rooftop" or "Rooftop Towncrier." He donned the toga of the African towncrier in his public discourses on social media, and in other public spheres as well, and understood what the literary critic Dan Izevbaye identifies as "the foregrounding of the public function of language" (15).

As a public intellectual, Adesanmi was never afraid to denounce Nigeria's socio-political decay as he named the dramatis personae in the political arena and spared no words in identifying "collaborators" and "sellouts." In one of the most searing passages in *You're not a Country, Africa!* (2011), he excoriates the "myth" of the "national cake" which he sees as "the operative national metaphor and one of the best explanations of our national tragedy" (202). Adesanmi writes:

> In essence, many aspects of our national malaise are tied to our loss of the struggle for meaning and there can be no respite until we understand the full ramifications of this phenomenon. Followership in Nigeria has been largely complicit in our losses in the field of meaning. We always wait for definitions to evolve from our contemptible ruling elite. The second phase emerges when the poltroons in the editorial rooms of the media regurgitate such brain-dead definitions of nationness. (202)

In his commentaries on social media and in his poetry, Adesanmi took to satire as leaves to a tree, to paraphrase the English Romantic poet, John Keats. He demonstrated awareness of the point made by Izevbaye that "the satirical option liberates the writer from the tragic implications of cyclical history" (22). As suggested above about his personal claim of a metaphysical *abiku* status, his writings were underlined by autobiographical tropes. From *You're not a Country, Africa!* through *Naija no Dey Carry Last* (2015) to the forthcoming posthumous collection of his keynote lectures *Who Owns the*

Problem? Africa and the Struggle for Agency (2020),[7] Adesanmi proved to be a master of his own narratives. He often spun seemingly minor everyday experiences in postcolonial Africa and in the Diaspora into large satirical statements about postcolonial politics of illusion and brutish existence. The seeds of such social consciousness were already sown in *The Wayfarer and Other Poems*—especially in the poems "Odia Ofeimun: The Brooms Take Flight" and "Message from Aso Rock to a Poet in Exile."[8] Given that his poetry collection is out of print, we have reproduced (with permission of his wife, Muyiwa) a selection in this anthology.

The Anthology

Wreaths for a Wayfarer is a tapestry of original poems by established and emerging writers from Africa and other parts of the world. In all, we received submissions from 257 writers from Nigeria, Ghana, Kenya, Zambia, Malawi, Tanzania, Uganda, Ethiopia, and South Africa. From outside of Africa, poets from Canada, Italy, The Netherlands, Sri Lanka, India, United Kingdom and the United States of America, also submitted towards the anthology. Interestingly, a 10-year old Nigerian-Canadian boy joined the league of poets who submitted poems for consideration for the anthology.

As editors, we were delighted by the number, diversity, and quality of the submissions. But we were saddened by the reality that we had to select 126 contributors out of the 257 submissions. A major challenge—which also happens to be a major strength of this anthology—is that we accepted submissions by budding poets. This necessitated editing and working with such authors to help develop writings that might otherwise have been rejected. The result is a collection that is a wide embroidery of poetic themes and forms from

---

7. The book is forthcoming under the imprint of Michigan State University Press (2020). However, all page references in this article is to the Feb 2019 version of the manuscript to which I had privileged access.
8. See the poems in Part IV of this anthology.

three generations of writers—from millennials to those born before and after the independence era of African countries, and reflecting the transnational connections of Adesanmi's life and work. While some of the poets memorialize Adesanmi, others philosophically reflect on existence, mortality, immortality and/or offer hope for the living, while avoiding hagiographies and panegyrics. We conceptualized an anthology that will be enduring in its thematic range and stylistic variety. And we got one; so that in this memorably textured collection, poets—who knew (or did not know) Adesanmi—exorcise the pains of loss through provocative poems that pour out their authors' beating hearts with passion.

This anthology is a cathartic exercise meant to contemplate the turbulence of death, as a way of seeking infinite relief or escape through writing. If, as the saying goes, life is not a laughing matter, one may ask, what then is death? The poets in this collection struggle with the riddle that life and death represent, and embrace the Siamese relationship between Death and Life, mourning and celebration:

> if you listen, you'd hear Nature speak
> of the eternal cycle: life and death[9]

Not unexpectedly, some of the poems are cries of anguish, others read like benedictions, while yet others are acclamations of *being* and *nothingness*.

While the anthology includes contributions by emerging poets, this volume features poems by well-known writers including Niyi Osundare, Akachi Adimora-Ezeigbo, Helon Habila, Jane Bryce, Uche Nduka, Peter Midgley, Afam Akeh, Chuma Nwokolo, Ian Keteku, Unoma Azuah, Emman Shehu Usman, Uzor Maxim Uzoatu, and Raphael d'Abdon. What unites them all, besides their thematic engagement with death, loss, and life, are the three "ems" that Paul Zeleza uses in describing third generation African writers: "multidimensionality, multifocality, and multivocality" (13). Holistically, the anthology is like a polyphonic orchestra, making sounds that echo our shared humanity. The capacity to make music out of tragedy seems natural to poets. Literary history

---

9. See Otiono's "After the funeral" in this volume.

is punctuated with elegies, dirges, hymns, sonatas, and cantatas dedicated to poets who died in their youth. Indeed, there seems to be a disquieting association between the powerlessness of human beings at an existential level, and the muse and mortality as evoked in the first epigraph to this Introduction. Still, we should remember the words of James Kaufman who, despite noting that "[t]he image of the writer as a doomed and sometimes tragic figure, bound to die young, can be backed up by research" (814), affirms that aspiring poets should not worry because "the fact that a Sylvia Plath or Anne Sexton may die young does not necessarily mean an Introduction to Poetry class should carry a warning that poems may be hazardous to one's health" (820).[10]

Our objective here was to transcend the gloom of tragedy to create a luminous celebration of life akin to the lively Festival of Life in Adesanmi's honor. The poets in this collection pride themselves in the *agency* that poetry as a mode of artistic and experiential expression offers. They exemplify the observation of Moore and Beier that: "To the African poet the dead will always remain near to the living 'like swimming mosquitoes in the evening', and he expresses the hope that even after death he will be close to the busy activities of this world" (13). So, rather than capitulate to the potency and inevitability of death, the poets deploy poetry to interrogate and resist it.

Recognizing, as did Wole Soyinka in *Poems of Black Africa* that "overlapping is obvious and frequent" (13) in anthologies of this nature, we have organized the poems into three main sections (Wayfarer, Requiems, and Homecoming), each reflecting the three stages of Adesanmi's life. The Wayfarer section contains poems that touch on the poet's peregrinations as explored in his poetry collection. The Requiem part represents the second phase of his development and features his lamentations about his homeland. The third part, Homecoming, includes poems associated with Adesanmi's tragic passing, or what in Nigeria's obituary discourses is also known as the "Home-call." In addition, we have included selections from Adesanmi's

---

10. For a related article see Idowu Omoyele's article, "*Death* Stalks *Nigeria's* writers." *Mail & Guardian*, February 17 2017, https://mg.co.za/article/2017-02-17-00-death-stalks-nigerias-writers.

The Wayfarer and Other Poems. Finally, we end with a section called Postlude.

Noteworthy about these phases is that in Adesanmi's death we find some parallels with the observations of Dan Izevbaye concerning Christopher Okigbo: "for what we encounter here is death as a passage, not an end" and "[t]his may be because he is essentially a poet of transition for whom death is not a final destination but only an archway" (24). Izevbaye also notes that Okigbo's "poems document his fatal fascination with death" (23). This, too, could be said of Adesanmi's poetry. A very close friend of Adesanmi's claims to have been with the poet one night when he suddenly woke up as if from a dream and wrote "Entries" while lamenting his concern over untimely death. The haunting closing lines of the poem have been chosen to close the selection from his own poetry collection in this anthology:

> Earthlings, among you I'm a prisoner of war
> Escape. Escape is always on my mind (60).

So powerful and so revealing is Adesanmi's friend's anecdote that it foregrounded the poem and contributed to my choosing it to read at the Festival of Life mentioned earlier. Interestingly, Adesanmi's students at Carleton University have reported his occasional introduction of his African Literature class at the beginning of the term by reading Wole's Soyinka's "Abiku" (J.P. Clark also has a poem with the same title), and foregrounding the spirit-child mystique and supernatural reincarnation by declaring that he, too, was an *abiku*! In fact, Adesanmi devotes Chapter One of his award-winning *You're Not a Country, Africa!* to discussing his abiku identity and how his beloved mother, Lois Olufunke Adesanmi, named him "Oota", meaning: "the symbolic stool on which she was finally able to sit securely in her husband's house" (8). Insightfully, in Adesanmi's poem "Entries," Baba Alabe finds the telluric antidote to the spirit-child who has many lives and is given to many exits and re-entries; he knows what needs to be done to make the spirit-child stay. Adesanmi identified the two short incisions (like the number eleven) on his cheeks as the symbol.

Several poets in this anthology—Usman Oladipo Akanbi, Ifesinachi Nwadike, and Kennedy Hussein Aliu & Leyda Jocelyn Estrada Arellano, and Adejumo Uthman Ajibola—explore the mysterious *abiku* lore. This mythopoeic dimension combines with the largely African cultural background of many of the contributors in this anthology to underscore the oral traditional roots of the poets. Thus, oscillating between the ancient and the modern, *Wreaths of a Wayfarer* echoes some pioneer anthologies of African poetry[11] while evoking the modernist temperament and style of Achebe and Okafor's *Don't Let Him Die*. What is more, some of the poems in this anthology are written in African languages or code-switching mode—with translation provided in some cases. Examples include Sihle Ntuli's "Scabha or The Sliding Door," Sunny Iyke U. Okeigwe's "Agadaga Iroko," Lebogang Disele's "Mogaka o ole", Kọ́lá Túbọ̀sún's "Akáṣọléri," and Susan Bukky Badeji's "The Water Pot is Broken." The use of traditional language, idioms and forms suggest that these emerging writers appreciate the necessity of preserving Africa-language literature or what the critic Oyekan Owomoyela identifies as "vernacular literature" (23) which he considered as being endangered.[12] Emmanuel Ngara foregrounds the significance of such use of tradition when he declares that "by using oral traditions as a means of communication the writer *ipso facto* helps to keep those traditions alive" (163).

The centrality of African tradition in this anthology reinforces and pays tribute to Adesanmi's immersion in the Yoruba worldview which he identifies as his "primary tool of analysis" (*You're Not a Country, Africa!* 179). In promoting the work of millennials in this anthology, we affirm the complex social milieu in which we live, and which frames this anthology. In their contributions to this anthology, poets such as Peter Akinlabi, Nkateko Masinga, Gbenga Adesina, Anushya Ramakrishna, Su'eddie Vershima Agema, Yejide Kilanko, Ejiofor Ugwu, and Razak Malik Gbolahan, offer readers a sampling of the cosmopolitan

---

11. The best known of the pioneer anthologies are: Olumba Bassir's *An Anthology of West African Verse* (1953) regarded as perhaps the first anthology of poetry published in Anglophone West Africa (Oyomolewa 2008: 8); Gerald Moore and Ulli Beier's *Modern Poetry from Africa* (1963); Ulli Beier's *African Poetry: An Anthology of Traditional African Poems*, Cambridge: Cambridge University Press, 1966; Donatus Ibe Nwoga's *West African Verse: An Anthology* (1967).
12. See chapters One and Two of Oyekan Owomoyela's *Africa Literatures: An Introduction*. Crossroads Press, 1979.

sensibilities of the emerging generation. Some others demonstrate audacious stylistic experimentation with form—Nathaniel Tanko Noah's "The Broken Quill," Bayowa Ayomide Michael's "Evening Bird," and Onuchi Mark Onoruoiza's "Homecall...047" and "Outshining the Stars." Inevitably, then, this anthology signals the work of this generation, highlighting the context in which Adesanmi poetically identifies with the emergent "hashtag generation" in *Who Owns the Problem?*:

> These, indeed, are great times to be a hashtag. In my second life, I'd prefer to come back not as a bird or a flower as is the wont of nature lovers but as the world's most recognizable symbol, the hashtag, previously only known to Americans and the English as the pound key on their phones but catapulted to planetary celebrity status in a little under a decade by Twitter. The hashtag is the only subject that can legitimately claim to be more famous than Kimye—that conjugal combination of Kim Kardashian and Kanye West. (11-12)[13]

Beyond the semiotic image of the "hashtag" as a signifier of Adesanmi's social media celebrity status with thousands of youthful followers from Nigeria and elsewhere on Facebook and Twitter, and his grounding in traditional African culture in his poetry and public commentaries, *Wreaths for a Wayfarer* offers an enduring platform for writers and readers to interrelate on the meaning of life and death. Tenibegi Karounwi's invocation of the multiple selves of the honoree of this book in his contribution to this anthology—"Pius: Myth, Mystic,

---

13. From the manuscript of *Who Owns the Problem?* Adesanmi provides more information about this chapter. According to him, "This keynote lecture was initially delivered as part of the opening session plenary addresses at the Fourth Annual Africa Renaissance for Unity Conference convened by the Africa Institute of South Africa and The Thabo Mbeki African Leadership Institute, Pretoria, South Africa, on May 22, 2014. A modified version of it was subsequently delivered as my valedictory lecture at the Institute of African Studies, University of Ghana, Legon, on May 29, 2014, in conclusion of my tenure as a Carnegie Diaspora Visiting Scholar."

Mystery"—rings so true about the overall intention of the anthology: "This is not a final curtain/ It is the beginning of remembering/ The birth of memories."

Works Cited

Achebe, Chinua and Dubem Okafor. Editors. *Don't Let Him Die: An Anthology of Memorial Poems for Christopher Okigbo, 1932–1967*. Enugu: Fourth Dimension, 1978.

Adesanmi, Pius. *Who Owns the Problem?: Africa and the Struggle for Agency*. Michigan State University Press, 2020.

———. *Naija No Dey Carry Last: Thoughts On A Nation In Progress*. Lagos: Parrésia Publishers Ltd. and Worldreader, 2016.

———. *You're not a Country, Africa!: A Personal History of the African Present*. Penguin Books, 2011.

———. *The Wayfarer and Other Poems*. Lagos: Oracle Books, 2001.

Aratani, Lori. "New lawsuit alleges that Boeing put profit over people with 737 Max." *Washington Post*, April 8, 2019. https://www.washingtonpost.com/local/trafficandcommuting/new-lawsuit-alleges-that-boeing-put-profit-over-people-with-737-max/2019/04/08/d93a7eba-5a36-11e9-a00e-050dc7b82693_story.html Accessed 12 August 2019.

BBC News. "Ethiopian Airlines: The Victims of a Global Tragedy." https://www.bbc.com/news/world-africa-47522028, April 4, 2019. Accessed 15 July 2019.

Beier, Ulli. Ed. *African Poetry: An Anthology of Traditional African Poems*, Cambridge: Cambridge University Press, 1966.

Clark, J.P-Bekederemo. "Abiku" *The Poems:1958-1998*. Lagos: Longman Nigeria Plc, 2002. p.6.

"FAA's Air Traffic Organization: Over 42,000 flights, 2.5 million passengers daily." ETurboNews, November 21 2018, https://www.eturbonews.com/238512/faas-air-traffic-organization-over-42000-flights-2-5-million-passengers-daily/. Accessed 9, July 2019.

Foucault, Michel. "What is an Author?" *Aesthetics, Method and Epistemology*. Ed. James D. Faubion. New York: The New Press, 1998.

Irele, Abiola. "The Development of Contemporary African Literature." *Authors: A Companion to Black African Writing (1300 to 1973),* Edited by Donald E. Herdeck, INSCAPE Corporation, 1970, pp. 481–86.

Izevbaye, Dan. "Living the Myth: Revisiting Okigbo's Art and Commitment." *Tydskrif Vir Letterkunde,* vol. 48, no. 1, 2011, pp. 13–25, doi:10.4314/tvl.v48i1.63817.

Kaufman, James C. "The cost of the Muse: Poets Die Young." *Death Studies,* vol. 9, pp. 813–21, 2003, doi:10.1080/713842357.

Keats, John. *The Letters of John Keats: Complete Revised Edition,* Edited by H. Buxton Forman. London: Reeves and Turner, 1895. pp. 93.

Mazareanu, E. "Number of Flights Performed by the Global Airline Industry from 2004 to 2020 (in Millions)." *Statista,* December 11 2019, https://www.statista.com/statistics/564769/airline-industry-number-of-flights/. Accessed 19 June. 2019.

Moore, Gerald and Ulli Beier. Eds. *Modern Poetry from Africa.* Middlesex: Penguin Books Ltd., 1963.

Ngara, Emmanuel. *Ideology and Form in African Poetry: Implications for Communication.* James Currey, 1990.

Nasir, Jamilah. "OBITUARY: In our hearts lies Pius Adesanmi, the prophet who foretold his Death." *The Cable,* March 12, 2019. https://www.thecable.ng/obituary-in-our-hearts-lie-pius-adesanmi-the-prophet-who-foretold-his-death Accessed 1 August. 2019.

Nwoga, Donatus Ibe. *West African Verse: An Anthology,* Humanities Press, 1967.

Nwokolo, Chuma. "An Epitaph for Pius Adesanmi" https://nwokolo.com/y/an-epitaph-for-pius-adesanmi/

Omoyele, Idowu. "Death stalks Nigeria's writers." *Mail & Guardian.* 17 Feb 2017. https://mg.co.za/article/2017-02-17-00-death-stalks-nigerias-writers Accessed 28 June. 2019.

Owomoyela, Oyekan. *The Columbia Guide to West African Literature in English since 1945.* Columbia University Press, 2008.

———. *African Literatures: An Introduction.* Crossroads Press, 1979.

Otiono, Nduka, Curator. "Festival of Life: In Honor of Pius Adesanmi." Carleton Dominion Chalmer's Centre, Ottawa, March 26, 2019.

———."The Night Hides with a Knife." *The Night Hides with a Knife.* Ibadan: New Horn Press and Critical Forum, 1995

———. "Swansong." *Camouflage: Best of Contemporary Writing from*

Nigeria. Edited by Nduka Otiono and Odoh Diego Okenyodo. Port Harcourt: Treasure Books, 2006, pp. 290-91.

Soyinka, Wole. "Abiku." *Idanre and Other Poems*. New York: Hill and Wangs, 1967, p.28

Yeats, William Butler. Ed. *Fairy and Folk Tales of the Irish Peasantry*. London: Walter Scott, 1888.

Zeleza, Paul. "Colonial Fictions: Memory and History in Yvonne Vera's Imagination." *Research in African Literatures,* vol. 38, no. 2, 2007, pp. 9–21, www.jstor.org/stable/4618370.

Introit: Coffin in the sky

NIYI OSUNDARE

(*Imagining how Oota*[1] would have contemplated the event of 03/10/19)

What song can one sing
   About that fruit
Which came down
   Too early, too unripe

How do we pen a paean
   For a promise
So cruelly spilled in the noon-
   Tide of a sky undone...

And the ashen anonymity
   Of the slaughter field
Its ruinous rainbow
   Its Golgotha of broken dreams

Whose hasty Science launched this coffin
   In the sky of our joy
To whose capital advantage do we owe
   This saga of endless anguish

Another star in our lifedance
   Done, mid-step, to a startled earth
We are too tired
   Of burying our best

Gone too soon
   But not before telling us all

---

1. A name of profound historical and familial significance that Pius's mother called him by, especially in moments of affectionate bonding.

How to wake the seed
    How to come to voice

PART I
WAYFARER

Scabha or The Sliding Door Operator

SIHLE NTULI

Scabha[1]

the way you personify the door,
shova imari ye phepha[2]
the human counter,
the clinging
the clanging sound,
the change
the tiny silver pieces.

your palm on the door
the way you smash the door
the sound it makes,
the brakes,
the quantum halts
from all your panel beatin',
industrial genre of music,
the door,
the dents you leave on
the door,
and so i ask
whose scars are these?

the way you let the commuter in
might you be,

---

1. isiZulu translation of door, also the colloquial name of the door man/taxi marshal responsible for operating the door and handling the money on behalf of the driver in a minibus taxi
2. "shuffle the banknotes" phrase inspired by the Bongo Maffin song 'Mari ye Phepha'

a projection of the cold wind
drifting in,
from the door
steel slides on steel,
unfolding your folding chair
you are self-sacrifice,
for the love of
the clinging
the clanging sound,
the change
the more things stay the same.

and about those small spaces in between chairs,
does it hurt when your body must fit there?
as you sit stand, stand sit,
or does it hurt more
that this is how you make your living.

there are signs of strength
and there are signs of weakness
shoulder
tensing,
clenching,
pushing,
full force,
the sound
when steel slides on steel,
the door slams shut!

facial clench,
eyeballs close,
shut tight
tucked inside
voice sinks,
the whisper,
my fear,
of death,
the interior,
a twenty-two-seater Quantum,

of all the places
that it could end.

sliding door operator,

in truth, it was I
who opened your door
from the outside,
in that single instant
like a predator
the door swallowed me,
with a sound
made by steel
when it slides on steel,
a thud,
when the door slammed shut,
the door now behind me,
and with that
safety grabbed
from my hands
and given
to God.

gentle easing of the lids
the eyeballs
and when my eyes open
they find you

sliding door operator,

with your cold face,
your cold stare,
as cold
and hard
as cash.

the way you personify the door,
opening and closing
that sound
when steel slides on steel

the door slamming shut
a sound of finality,

sliding door operator

how do you keep so cool?
how do you remain unperturbed?
then it occurs to me
how you may already
be ready,
or could it be,
that finally
you are death.

When an Iroko Falls

IQUO DIANA ABASI

...in lieu of a wreath

When an Iroko falls,
the land trembles in awe,
young and old gather,
tell tales, not tall,
of might and stoicism,
admiration of a fine-ness
too glaring to be captured in words.

A fearless Iroko sapling lies prone,
the lips of this child are ill-prepared
for panegyrics, yet she attempts;
like teeth hard pressed to chew water,
like a babe learning to bathe,
she succeeds by washing the belly squeaky clean.

The spear was heavy but
you wielded it bravely,
piercing falsehood with precision
per time, who now will wield this lance?
whose humour will henceforth dispense
laughter and intent musing?

But who are we to complain
when the drumbeats stop
while the next step is suspended mid-air,
the next love letter to motherland,
but a rapidly cascading whorl
of thoughts, hopes, dreams.

Your sojourn did not end, wayfarer,
only your location and audience changed,
your roots sank far here, tendrils birthed courage,

but others rejoice in realms yonder,
for a fine human has returned to whence
he once sought leave to go share his gifts.

May your journey not end wayfarer,
till you are blazing light,
an unstoppable illuminant,
polished and clarified gem,
a true warrior,
swinging aloft in eternal bliss

How to Survive War in Nigeria

IQUO DIANA ABASI

Order a beer and spiced meat,
watch the razing of whole villages,
shake your weary head,
shrug your secure shoulders,
wish the northerners well.

Four years post-Chibok
argue that it is a farce still,
propaganda from the opposition, to
undermine the government of your brother
from another tribe in the south.

Hear of flags hoisted in the North East,
claim this is karma, served hot,
for the death of your brothers and
sisters for decades on end,
in the name of religion.

Laugh off Mubi, Baga, Bama, Gwoza,
say 'Na dem-dem, e no konsain us!'
flip the channel, seek Serie A, La Liga,
EPL & Champions league on Supersport,
order some peppersoup,

Write off Dapchi,
argue about Leah,
'How are we sure the abductions happened'?
Claim it was all staged to make the
government appear to be working.

Shout yourself hoarse at the killing
of a Christian evangelist.

Raise hell only when churches
are bombed in the north, look away
when the victim is a non-Southerner.

Grimace at the execution of Leman,
Ask no one in particular
'These people are still at it?'
learn some shaku-shaku,
keep the hustle on full throttle.

One half of Nigeria may be in a chokehold,
but you club hard and stay 'woke'.
people may fear to travel or farm
from village to village, but for you,
life on cruise control is no adage.

I Wet the Earth, I Sing You Wreaths...

FAREED AGYAKWAH

March 10, 2019:
The world's wide ears
Didn't receive the sweetest
Feathers of news—
"Pius Adesanmi passes on."

When decayed comets of pilots
Mistake aircrafts for vans
Such sad passing, Pius,
Without a goodbye kiss,
Without a last prayer,
Breaks the heart of the Earth.

Writer, scholar, educator,
The seed of your passing
Didn't fall on the ripest
Soils of the heart.
"Pius Adesanmi passes on?"

When corrupt officials
Cut the corners of due diligence
Such salt-spilling, Pius,
Without a warm embrace,
Without a final handshake
Blinds the sight of the World.

However, we try to turn it,
The ear drum protests like a rifle,
Hearts bleed profusely like a sacrificed pigeon
On the sad news of meteoric passing.
"Pius Adesanmi passes on?"

Wayfarer, Payo de Pius,
Pius whose basket holds all waters,
Pius at the 47th parallel of handsomeness,
With some one hundred and fifty-six souls
You cross the Mediterranean of life
I wet the Earth; I sing you wreaths.

Harvest IV

FUNMI ALUKO

I am a message
Listen!
I'm Afuape
The message lies in the lyrics
Of primordial drumming
Loud and resolute

I am seed
Canal of inspiration
Component of coupling desires
Requisite for germination
Ally of moisture
A friend of rain

I am harvest
Consequence of the till
Yield of the sowing
Strength of the grind
Gathering of the crops
Evidence of a season

I am joy
Of seed time and harvest
A fistful of sunflowers
A well of abundance
Crust, mine, treasure

I am an angel
A tree in the desert
A succor south of the Sahara
A response to the famine
Of the spirit

I am Afuape

    The message
        The lyrics of primordial drums
            Loud and resolute!

Wayfarer

FUNMI ALUKO

A thousand steps
Rolling
Shifting
Splattering

A thousand steps I hear
Shifting and splattering
Rolling resonating rhythms
Like beats
On Bata drums

A thousand steps I hear
Splattering loud and fast
Littering the streets
With anxious moves
Searching a pseudo
searching tomorrow

I'm a rider with restful spirit
Riding…

Dawn after dawn, riding
Riding

If tomorrow comes
Riding…

The Wayfarer

SAUDAT SALAWUDEEN

Travellers, each strapped to his back
his life's worth and when he'll be back

On this path legs unknown work
and each tied to its own dinging clock

like an athlete's legs yawning for trophy
life isn't such to live in a hurry

every leg strives to cross that Rubicon
but only a few brace selves for the fall

and thrive defying thorns' foils
where others break stance and loss

Which head doesn't desire a crown?
What eye wouldn't like an ocean of fans?

Every man his own boss and worth
like the price tag for his gut and all

Travellers, each on a mission,
the one who bears the cross is you.

End of Forever

SAUDAT SALAWUDEEN

There's a crown
that fits every head—
it is death
don't moan
There's a colour
that suits every skin—
it is death; my kin
don't get sore

There's a shelter with a
single entrance, six feet deep
everybody must sleep till the
end of forever

Muse of Homecoming

JUSTUS K. S. MAKOKHA

The heart often wants to flee home
In search of that beyond the horizons[1]

Sometimes the crave sires the crazy
Like serpents sire themselves by skins

The mind is torn from its restful axis
Rotates on the bases of restlessness

Vomit-like venom sears the arteries
Pumping wanderlust even in testicles

The itch becomes unbearably strong
Long as the feet remain planted here

With the palm a shield against fears
Known and unknown, you face there

You face there with reptilian intention
Eyes asquint under the tropical skies

Mirages rise as like dust of an accident
To show black scars, each, a souvenir

Black is the heart and the awakened brain
In such moments of artful rememory…

And when Abroad, finally, unclasps you
Wanderer lust, you'll feel it in you again

The sound of the broken minarets, yes
Sounds of home slithering into your Life!

---

1. *Muse of Homecoming* is excerpted from a four-part sequence.

Sounds that recite the quatrains of here
Where you left a sandal as you flee here

Where the sandal still slides like dunes
Dancing to tunes of gunshots and hyenas

It is true that the memory is sad and plain
Yet it'll never go, long as you flee yourself

And like the sandal that you left in the sun
Refusing to die with plastic litter of Ethiopia

Refined our parable praising the sun which set
...as did Somalia, yet, in the East rise...it shall

Again and again, from Meccaaa to Americaa
And from lands of peace...to ours of...woes...

Encore

AGATHA AGEMA

this sound that you hear/ like a rumble in the distance/no
it is not the sound of thunder/it is the crushing weight/of a continent's worth of wailing
of wailing/for a kernel of hope/crumbled in the dust.

the hands that cupped the flame/grew weary in the first watch/of the morning
grew weary and fell/ not weightless, to the dust/ raised a phantom fled away
on the wings of an eastern morning/a blaze of light eternal/to mark its path.

(Pause)

they say that when the bud is green/yet falls from the branch/at its tender tip
then the roots have dried of sap/that the flower will not appear/that the drought
will lick the leaves/and sear their green to gold/and turn the hope of food to dust.

we went posthaste/teeth on edge, with trepidation/to the place
where the meteorite kissed the earth/a searing kiss/that blacked the ground
where the comet lost its tail/turned the face of heaven grey/to dispute the stories we had heard.

but the wayfarer/his face was janus/his tongue, the sphinx
met our handshake with a scythe/harvested our hearts/on broken prayer beads
reaped from us/ a basketful of tears/at sunset's edge.

and from the ashes/shall rise again/thousand phoenixes – feathers bright
a million flowers, joyous spring/a harvest of colors/an offering

song
from rich dark earth/made moist with blood/of fount that slaked a million thirst.

Now that I know young birds die in flight

SEGUN MICHAEL OLABODE

Pius, I am at your funeral with a coffin to bury
My own wings.

The orange tree sprouting from my father's land
of greed withered before it bore half its fruits and I realise
I am still a man of my world with two ordinary lungs, a dark continent,
sea eyes and legs walking midriff in my own grave.

Wayfarer, that uncompromised light exposing in light speed
the financiers of our chains and the alcoves of their diggings,
exposing all the native wolves yanking apart the bowels of a people's hope.
Pius, "one man against the authorities," one man for his country
a press of thorns in the ass of corruption and its black ass agents.

In the hollow of an eternal night a name peddles itself from mouth to mouth
like a song on a plantation field, we sing it for a song is its own voice
we sing it and a rainbow 'Pius' our shredding sky.

I shall spend the next two centuries building
a coffin big enough to contain your oblivion or the name of your African country. Building, building and building,
echoes of your voice reluctantly hinging the planks together and the hammer
taking years in descent.

In the end of time it will be your funeral finally and the field will be a cemetery
of coffins, each mourner lowering something of themselves into

your grave
until the land becomes a tower of deadness resurrecting in your name
because some suns, except it's the end of time, don't ever set
or why die when you cannot be raised back to life in songs or poems,
our Pius lives on, a song that peddles itself from mouth to mouth,
light in the heart of darkness.

The Water-Pot is Broken

SUSAN BUKKY BADEJI

(*Alternatingly: Crier and Chorus*)

>Cutting through the belly of the fast-fading dawn
>Feet a-wash with sobs of the night before
>
>Night insects, from approaching dusk, take flight,
>Fleeing from, and flirting with, the emerging light.
>
>Late night owls hoot to their human form,
>Or never to form will they return.
>
>In frightening howls, they breeze in flight,
>Before the sun opens its striking eyes.
>
>Wet, mourning leaves their feet crush,
>Pot-bearers heed the river's dawn call.
>
>Sharp and piercing cry, the air it rends,
>Travelling fast to the jungle's ends.
>
>Interjecting the river's glorious hush,
>Ululation to her waking ears rush.
>
>A pot-bearer writhes in wailing pangs,
>Singing in pain a dirge someone sang.
>
>Osan ja, orun d'opa[1]
>Broken string turns the bow to a plain stick.

---

1. *Osan* and *Orun* are Yoruba words for the materials used to design a bow (Bow and Arrow). *Orun* is a flexible stick; osan is the string that holds the stick in place when bent. When the string breaks, *osan* snaps back into an ordinary stick.

Eti ge, ori d'apola igi![2]
Missing ears turn the head to a tree!

The water-pot breaks, the water spills,
Forty-seven seasons and the pot sighs.

Eyes crimson with tears unshed,
Men loiter in homesteads with drooping heads.

Hunter dogs snarl in mournful drawl.
Trees tumultuous, wail the night before.

Cooking pots blackened with soot and smoke
Lay scattered in chaos as the sun rises at dawn.

---

2. *Eti* and *ori* are Yoruba words for ear and head, respectively. *Apola igi* is literally translated as tree-trunk or plank. Yorubas believe that the ears are not just for hearing, but also aesthetic, and actually defines the head. When the ears are missing, the head loses its definition. The two lines are used to express dismay, sorrow, agony and a deep sense of loss and hopelessness.

from absence, memory and farther

OBEMATA

1
after the road departed,
taking you by the hand
the earth turned away
and took rivers with it,
leaving us with the wind,
life wounded by absence.
then the wind turned away,
leaving sad murmurs
in the ears of sad birds
hidden inside memories.
then the birds disappeared,
fastening memories
to the yolks of eggs
laid on long suffering grass.
the birds have flown.
the grass has turned away,
returning its suffering to headstones
that aren't tired of mourning.
wayfarer, since you left,
i forge keys from the earth,
turn the locks of the world
to bless those who mourn.

2
on this side of absence
is silence, space, darkness,
spread like a scar over an old wound.
this silence hurts so i wander
away from the darkness of death
in grief, to look for reprieve, surfeit of light,

finding only faces lost in sunset, louder
in silence, in voids, filled with voids, voices
in search of voices that lose their way
in the music of silence
overhanging the cathedral of mourners,
where hurt is as sad as sadness,
as the psalm someone mutters to himself.
on this side of absence is darkness,
scattered ashes, death that can no longer
take the life it has already taken,
or extinguish my memory of the poet,
who, like Secundus, has taken a vow of silence.
i look at the space. i call light out of darkness.
the louder i call, the louder silence answers me.

3
wait, wait, wait for me, you said.
i waited for you
till i disappeared into sadness
reborn as absence
in the houses of absence, without presence,
in the storehouses of ripened hunger,
in lonely cities, lonelier with loneliness,
in the streets of sadness
that everyone arrives sad and departs saddest,
by the river emptying
itself of sand and stones,
weeping on a barren
patch that sings of its barrenness
to sand and stones.
wait for me, you said. i waited for you, and i am still waiting.
in this endless wait,
my heart longs for you.
this wait that waits for itself,
for you and weights my heart
is a spot on memory.
i cling to memory, sadness sunders us.
wait for me, wait for me, wait for me, you said.

Umbilicals

TIJAH BOLTON-AKPAN

Isanlu
Today, your leafless trees speak of lifeless birds
Speak truth
To a country some named Africa

Unwelcome,
Home becomes
The theatre of jollof rice wars
Shame settles scores between pride and longing
And the shower head
Becomes the parable

We have forged joys
Over fights, over words
Not for ourselves,
But for the lie we nicknamed a country
Words have consumed us
As we pushed in birth pangs
From the windy womb of the prophecy

This is for you, Wayfarer
This is for the testaments to broken dawns
The restless spirit has flown away
Who will tame our demented king?

This is for you, Wayfarer,
This is for the tomorrows you dared to build
When we quarrel over places that divide us
Who will heal the broken bones with a bandage of laughter?
This is for Omoluabi
Umbilicals in a common earth
May this journey
End better than it began

The Pilgrim Unbound

CLARA IJEOMA OSUJI

Silence.
The storm comes
Not a soul of the 157 stirring
Amidst tufts, clatters and smothering
The voyagers lie in charred rubbles.
The Erudite explorer rouses unbound
Beholding the gloomy ascending horizon
In the bleak still seconds of the seething craft
Bravely rides the wind heavenward.

Six minutes lethal ascent
Bishoftu environs vibrate
More silences; no remnant voices
To tell the tale of the pious pilgrim.
The narrative of mortal existence is grim
Crowded with entrances and exits,
Appearances and disappearances
Arrivals and departures

Hush.
After the storm
The restless quester; the erudite wanderer
Swiftly discerns the smoldering wreckage
And soars resiliently to celestial heights
Through the placid pre-noon air
Unfettered by human frailties.
Arrives at that Golden City, sculpted by God;
Infinite, boundless, liberated
The unbound pilgrim has triumphed.

The human resolve to grasp
To untangle the tale of the storm
The computer versus man narratives

Prick our very souls, offer no respite.
This bizarre conflict between man and machine?
Noisy infuriating explanations
Fail to assuage our angst
Tender no comfort to our pangs.

More noises.
Automated safety system – maneuvering,
And sorely Nigeria mourns
Her Poet, Essayist, Academic and Activist.
The dialectics of wrong sensor reading
Becomes undesirable noise to a grieving nation
Tales of false automated safety deciphering
A tug of war between craft and crew;
The craft prevails over crew
Automated massive obliteration
Unrecoverable nosedive
Fiery fatal plunge

Impermanence.
Addis Ababa to Nairobi
Death veiled in a connecting flight
Flies the scholar into new Intellectual range
Though death has its day
Pious thoughts profound, deep
As the sea – the pilgrim demonstrates
Confidence that he has a Life when
His sojourn on this earthly plane is done
And takes to heart the biblical Psalms via
That foreboding signing out: Psalm 139:9-10
Affirming faith in His Guiding Right Hand.

Indignant.
We hope it didn't happen
Yet, here we are –
Friends, admirers and fans
Now after the storm
Bereft of coherent answers, still absorbing the shocks,

But scripting our debts of earnest homages
Our reverential dirges for the unbound sage

Remarkable affinities of arrivals and departures
The pilgrim-child arrives this mortal plane on Sunday
Coincidentally, the Sunday child departs on another Sunday
47 years making history and laurels
A yam tendril, pledging
Wavering resolutely in the wind
Snapping too soon.
Superior excellence;
Magical erudition – clarity of the pen
More known in death than in life

Bustles.
Movements, travels and returns
Arrivals and departures
Now unfettered by mortal frailties,
Finally, free from earthly strife
The scholar, son, brother, father and husband
Does take the wings of that Sunday morning
Not to dwell in the uttermost parts of the sea
But skyward to the Guiding Hands of his maker
The Knowledge-Producer now returns.

Not one, but all 150 Psalms eternally to sing.
Interminably pacing that Street of Gold
Psalming for all eternity the Majesty
Of the King of all, the Great I Am.
To the unbound soul, the erudite pilgrim
From this material plane
We dauntlessly intone:
Farewell mortality,
Welcome immortality!

Eclipsed at Noon

ABDULAZIZ ABDULAZIZ

For Pius Adesanmi

    In the fullness of the noon
    Storms
    Lightning
    Storms
    The rising sun is eclipsed.
    In the fullness of the noon

    The desert rose blossoms
    In the dryness of the land
    It blossoms
    Though the dictator refuses to water
    Still it grows—a darling for all.

    The mother cow is felled down
    What befalls its sucking calves?

    The winged machine growls
    The tall daisy is mowed.
    We mourn.

To the Daughters

ABDULAZIZ ABDULAZIZ

The antelope doesn't spend a lifetime running
And its child crawls

Pick up the tools he left—
The grassland he left untilled
Is your field to till
The words he left unsaid we wait to hear you say
The work he left undone is yours to do

Take the name he left at home
Weave it around the shoulders
Strut the stage high up
Dad's brightened the dais for you.

The Traveler

ABIODUN BELLO

Earth...
Rain...
Earth and rain
For your passage,
You who knocked
The door of Death
In the morning...

The morning rain
Rattled the dry soil
And knitted the leaves
Beneath the dew
And settled the stirring dust
That would shut your eyelids
Eternally!

Dust to dust
And ashes to ashes
You made your house
With Death
And ate your yam with our Dead
Even before your time

Pius!
The earth must
Sharpen its hatchet
And carve new hilts
And build up
Your forsaken ridges
At the last place
Of your early ploughing

Now you walk through
Your passage of time—

Eternal time—
Take this lamp
And this oiled wool
That you may tread on,
And travel this road
Of lights and shadows
As your kith
Lay down
These flowery wreaths
Over your lowered head
O young wayfarer!

For the Wayfarer

CHIFWANTI ZULU

Those who knew Payo would bear witness
That there was not a life more fabled than his
That even as the world was wowed by the magic of his pen
He always took pride in the Naija flag and his countrymen
That he was truly a man of character and vision
And once committed he stood by his decisions
And from these commitments many lives were touched
On March 10th even more hopes and dreams were crushed
Flamboyantly, his wandering spirit rose and in silence fell
Now let us lay the wreaths and tell the wayfarer's tale.

The Acts of Brother Pius

'BUNMI OGUNGBE

"what did you think?"
he threw back his head and laughed in that way of his,
with abandonment, but hollow this time
teeth, white, fresh, like the *nunu*[1] sold in calabashes on Lokoja highway
skin, rich, immaculately dark, just like *koro isin*[2]
"what did you think?
that i would go without a roar?
that the sun would not eat itself?
that the moon would not swallow itself up in agony?
that i would be silent?
well, now you sure know better!"
he glanced away in disgust

"you should ask Mama Adesanmi how i came here?
she will regale you with stories of my infantile ebullience
i am too extraordinary to go silently
was I silent when i had warm blood?" He turned
"how could you even think that i will be in death?
just how nah?" He laughed that hollow laugh again.

"rock back and forth for a minute,
do you see what i saw?" he whispered
"do you feel that gnawing silence that thrusts my jaw open every time?
so then you cannot be silent!" He pointed his finger
"do not dare!" He raised his voice this time
"speak up to that continent,

---

1. A milk product (yoghurt-like) commonly sold by West African Fulani women.
2. The black seed of the Ackee fruit (*Blighia sapida*), the entire phrase is a yoruba simile.

write it, dance it, speak it, tweet it,
play it, post it, sing it, publish it,
just never let the silence be what is!
i don't care if all you can mutter is about the potholes on the road to Isanlu,
i may laugh at your ignorance,
but i will stand proudly at your courage to speak."

"Tise..." His features softened.
"she will know." He was barely audible
"she will find me within herself, where i always will be."

"it is
it is done
i was, and i will be."

Backing His Daughter: For Pius, on Facebook

JANE BRYCE

What does it mean when
a man
ties his daughter to his back?
Wraps himself in a wrapper
lets himself
be late for work
undoes
knots of tradition
unravels
mysteries of fatherhood?

Will his daughter remember when,
later,
she stands at the plinth,
the lectern,
the bridal altar,
the back that carried her?

Will she, fumbling the knots of her wrapper,
feel the tied traces
of a lost love?

Backing her own baby,
will she feel her father's heart
beat in her own breast?

Avoiding Sunlight

UNOMA AZUAH

I can't stay for too long in these tunnels avoiding sunlight
cringing at every explosion that flies past my eyes
I can't stay in these tunnels for too long
subdued by sounds of crickets shrilling
to placate the night that has befallen us
I can't stay in these tunnels for too long
gagging at the stench of these trenches
Here corpses are clustered around broken things
each piece cries
I can't stay in these tunnels for too long
scorpions claw at cold air
even gnats brace for the pain
The reign of ashes has infiltrated
every space that breathes
And life, like the floating feathers of blasted birds, has been blown to bits
I can't.
How do I gather these pieces of flesh
To find a pulse in this body that has deluded me
A body too heavy to be lifted.
This body has become a burden to be laid to rest.

Akáṣọlérí (Mourners)

KỌ́LÁ TÚBỌ̀SÚN

Fún Àwa tó Ṣẹ́kù

Táa bá ń sunkún kálé
Ṣebí t'ara wa la rí wí
Ìgbà tí a bá ń dárò ká'jà
Ọ̀rọ̀ ara wa gan la ń rò
Ọmọ Adésanmí ti ná'jà
Ó ti k'ẹ̀rùu oko ẹ re'lé lọ
Kí wá la wá ń dami lójú
Poroporo fún gan-an?

Ibi ayé bá ti ká ni mọ́
Ibẹ̀ la ti ń jẹẹ́ tipẹ́tipẹ́
Bẹ́ẹ̀, ibi ìpẹ̀kun bá ti dé
bá ni lọ́dẹ̀dẹ̀ ọ̀gànjọ́
báa fẹ́, báa tiẹ̀ kọ̀,
Ibẹ̀ náà làá f'àdàgbá rọ̀.
Èwo wá ni igbe, ariwo yaya
Omijé ojúu wa?

Ẹkún ara wa la ń sun
Òògbé ara wa là ń tọ̀
Iṣẹ́ ọwọ́ọ wa la ń wò
Láwòdunra — omi adágun
Ayé lá ṣánpá sí
Táa ló fẹ́ gbé wa lọ.
Ìhòhò ara wa lo hàn tán
Táa fẹ́ f'ìdárò bò mọ́lẹ̀.

Mourners

For us who remain

When we cry around the house
Aren't we asking about our own fate?
While we cry in pain around the market
It's our own circumstance we're pondering?
The son of Adésanmí has prowled the market
And has now carried his purchased goods homewards
So why the torrent of tears
That flood from all our tired eyes?

We are compelled, by life's caprice,
To enjoy life, when we can, where we can.
And when the inevitable end arrives,
Even if by the sacred midnight,
Whether we like it or not,
We suspend all actions and go with it.
So, why the wailing, the loud crying,
The hot restless tears?

We are merely crying for ourselves
We slumber for our future sleep.
It is the work of our hands that we stare at
wistfully — the restful lake of our lives
We're gesturing towards, nervously,
Worried that it would sweep us away.
Perhaps it is our nakedness now exposed
That we wish to cover with our loss.

Last Tweets

KỌ́LÁ TÚBỌ̀SÚN

Òkú ń sunkún òkú
Akáṣọlérí ń sunkún ara wọn

Because we do not know
which is the last collection
we'd take from the public
cooperative, or the last piece
of clothing, freshly sewn,
that will remain unused on our
shelves when we step out
into the cold morning air
and into the arms of waiting
history, we say our goodbyes
in every tweet, every like, every
wave and thumbs thrown
into conversations never concluded,
projects never finalized, meetings
never actualized over distances
drawn by fate and time.

Because we do not hear
the farewells in the laughters
drawn on our quotidian chores,
the pain filtered through every visa
wait, and security check and pat downs
through Ethiopia and Istanbul and
Heathrow and Paris; and in the
shrugs we substitute for commentary
when the weight of circumstances
push us into the hammock of curated silence,
we settle for hugs and bubbles
of thought in each other's' way
when their face flies into our view

on a quiet night, when the last
thing we wanted to hear was
"Didn't I see him just last…"

Because we do not know
on whose head the sequined cap
that finally caught up with Aríkúyẹrí
will land next, in the weight
of its inevitability, drawn from
close shaves, miracle saves,
mothers' prayers, missed appointments
and all vain escapes we praise
in songs and dance and poems
and creative pretences to permanence,
we draw our breaths with fire
and blood, rumble through the earth
with the passion of gods
with loud bells and talking drums
on their heels like kings, like men
unafraid of the memories we weave.

Farewell, Wayfarer

OYINKANSADE FABIKUN

I once knew a wayfarer,
He came from the city of Confluence
From the womb of a giant he emerged
Like the rising sun, steady was his appearing and welcoming was his warmth
For the quest of knowledge, he went westward and westward
He savored a strange tongue and took it to heart
As a compass guides the traveler,
So did the new tongue guide the wayfarer
Farewell, wayfarer,
Travel far and travel wide
But never forget the home where your heart beats.

I once knew a wayfarer,
He voyaged from the belly of a giant
Until he came to the place of the maple
To rise above equals and to take up the staff of an erudite giant
Up and up went the wayfarer, shining brighter and brighter
But why does your heart still ache for home oh wayfarer?
Why do you speak still for the speechless?
How are you so far and yet so near?
Farewell, wayfarer,
Fly far and soar high
But never forget the home where your heart beats.

I once knew a wayfarer,
He traveled to the ends of the earth
To the places we know until he arrived at a place of no return
We see his compass, we see his tools but we can't see the wayfarer
Who has set him who traveled hills and valleys?
Who lent his voice to the voiceless?
Has his breath gone with the wind?

Has his voice been silenced in sleep?
Has he drawn the curtains while it is yet day?
Farewell, oh wayfarer,
Travel up and travel northwards
But never forget the home from which your path originated.

Solitaire

KAFILAT OLOYEDE

Me a recluse? Far from it!
Pezophaps' fate I sure reject.
But this puzzle alone I must sort
Singing soulfully while doing the catch
May be deficient in looks or stretch
But my song your soul will lift

Solitaire is the game of life.
The game of life is solitaire
Life's puzzles in different colours
And strength you must sort.
Ordering and ranking the cards I'm dealt
Hoping my best will be good enough

When at start easy is the game
You walk and stroll like a maestro
Then difficulty level changes
You scratch your head and roll in bed
Then shine the rays of a bright new dawn
Thank goodness, the monster is gone.

Then like in school, you need some height,
Another set of tests of you required
Difficulty level changes to high
You try all the tricks to trick the trial
You hire old skills to shuffle and reshuffle
Unyielding remains the puzzle

But life is no pile of cards to flip over.
The reserve cards having run out and
Retrieving from the discard pile impossible,
With the puzzle getting knottier
I deal again.

How to Keep the Wake for a Shooting Star

CHUMA NWOKOLO

grief
is optional.
do they not know?
that the destiny of a
shooting star is
brevity?
you
chose
this path,
primed your
rockets. your day
arrives, clothes your
plane in splendour. this
is your cause: blaze a path
in darkness, do they not know?
now, darkness stars ignited faces:
despair's excluded. do they
not see? the smiles that
attend the wake of
shooting stars?
the uplifted
hearts,
upturned
countenances?
you chose to prod
a complacent cosmos, to
pique conceit, to trigger thought.
in your wake, a despondent universe
does not resume: see, the illumined faces.
shooting stars die, to blaze on in men's hearts.

Eagle

UZO ODONWODO

> *Porque una negra noche se accumula en la boca?*
> *Porque muertos?*
> Why must the blackness of nighttime collect in our mouths? Why, the dead?
> —Pablo Neruda, "There's No Forgetting."

Sadness removes the blanket of blackness over the palm-wine dawn
Thirsting for genius blood, ancient Ethiopian hills yearn gory libations

The first meeting was the last. The stage was
Winter-weary East Lansing bleeding snow

In the womb of the metal bird made of the mortal hands of man
You saw the future first and curled in the nest that was God

The room was peopled with those huddled at your feet, Oluko
In your voice, the authority of a Pentateuchal prophet

Rich as verdant prose, this life, short as a telegram
You were like a comet over our nightsky

Nigeria: a vista of decadence: pharaohs over a desolate wasteland
So many bodies missing, cemeteries scattered, marked & unmarked plots

Happen you come to the crepuscular calm of the crossroads
Choose the grassy footpath to the cavern of Mother Idoto

Chocked quiet, loss flaps his hands in our heaving hearts
You tried, you tried to boot us awake

Ascend now in the dew of this culpable morning
On the wings of birds that do not fail

We left the beer and banter for the next time
I bear now as a scar the hurt of that missed bottle

You soared into the sorry endlessness of the orange sunrise
You, eagle, made of the immortal hands of God.

In Memoriam

UZO ODONWODO

> Come Lord, and lift the fallen bird
> Abandoned on the ground;
> The soul bereft and longing so
> To have the lost be found.
> — T.Merrill, "Come Lord And Lift."

You were an eagle made God
Unblemished plumage with all the glory of flying
A pen was a whip, was a thorn in your hands,
Was a flying missile since it has always been
Mightier than a sword in the scabbard
And as hawks fly down & rip innocent chicks from their mothers
This metal vulture made from the mortal hands of man has
Ripped you from the warm hug of your mourning mother
Even though you were not a hawk
Even though you were an eagle made of the hands of God

You were an eagle made God
A vista of decadence, a wasteland of rapacious leaders
From your perch you saw the future first and spat your disgust
We, slaves of these merciless pharaohs you cursed,
We huddled at your feet, Oluko, and with your hands
You fed us the wisdom to boot us all awake.
And now we see, we see it clearly:
So many bodies missing, cemeteries scattered, marked & unmarked plots
So many people hungry, so much rage, so much sadness, so much tears
So many hopeless & crying, so many lost, so many so many!
Stop and think about it for a minute: the pointlessness of it all.
You saw and spat your disgust & you soared into the sorry endlessness of the orange sunrise
For you were an eagle made God.

Can You Do This Thing?

SARAH KATZ-LAVIGNE

Can you do this thing?

—Buy these apples and bananas (four of each)
—Ride this bus
—Meet your mother (at her house)
—Sit, sit, sit, stare:
that person's leather gloves, his "stylish" rubber boots
black with a lining of cloth

—the list goes on and on

the mind, too, gets scorched
like the sun-dripped field
scorched by jet fuel

but the mind never stops
never creeps into silence

it never falls still.
but only stops imagining
for a time

only builds a temporary shelter
incomplete
and not hardy enough
for a winter
or a forest fire.

the signs of weakness are there
if you know where to look

watching this video about homeless dogs,
and their people
the few tears leaking out
before you stop them up

mostly, there are signs in silence.
a thousand people
—maybe 1005
—maybe a lot more
　going around, and about
—on the bus
head propped against a
dusty sunlit window,
rarely cleaned

Asking themselves:
Can I do this thing?
this thing I have to do—

without him

This mundane thing, today.
Like crossing the snow-mush street
Like seeing my mother

Not knowing that they can
But knowing they will

And never speaking of grief.

Lights

JOHN CHIZOBA VINCENT

Last night, we saw god remove this:
blood-stained clothes from the sky,
burnt ashes & dust of men of great honour,
he bridled their housed tears almost home
& their memories, he lost in abyss of death.
this is how death guided their hope in tears
& the only pictures seen are restlessness.
Sometimes our bodies melt away from
the salvations of humanity & sacrilegious
spirits & our reflections become scary,
we fold ourselves into brown sorrow like
we'll return here with a sermon of divinity
to redemption, to reconnect those lost in
between fate & destiny & search for freedom.
But
Life is a boring adventure keeping watch
over the tragedies of death & those killed.
every room becomes available for shadows,
black tilted shadows. broken. Teared up.
having the memories & reflections of life,
Bodies burnt by fire, bodies swallowed, bodies
slaughtered; bodies wounded, & those taken.
Journey's full of meanings and mysteries,
feeding its eyes with nightful of uncertainty.
Emeka was engulfed yesterday in an autocrash,
His mother planted a forgotten kiss on altars,
Femi was slaughtered by lurking herdsmen,
He never returned from farm & family waited,
Musa admired the sun & was gunned down,
We gather these memories at dawn for Pius
'cause we never know who returns every time.
His deeds will linger from those red flames

raising his names before the lazy clouds to light up the world from the face of the Earth.
I'm sure god wears him like a prayer,
I'm sure he held these lights flags of heroes closer to him even as he drowned in himself.
Let these lights keep his memories in our palms till tomorrow when next we meet.

The Meteorite

OMOWUMI OLABODE STEVEN EKUNDAYO

In their flights over the sky
meteors burn bright and brief.
Keen, deep and long is this grief
that makes us rue and cry
for the sudden crash of a meteorite.
Payo, how did you become that slight
fall of hailstone held between two fingers on high
that dropped on an overheated pan of hell
which now makes us writhe and yell?

Death is the villain that broke in at night
and stabbed your heart deep
while you were resting in the bosom of sleep
and anon, our mirth was microwaved into a blight.
With surrender, the rising sun set at noon
and eclipse blackened our diurnal boon.
Why were you not the canary in a swift flight
who jammed no tree till he returned to his nest?
Should the ripening coconut drop ere harvest?

Lo! Mother Sky is lonesome without her escorting cloud
and her Sister-Earth glowers at her for rain
to soothe her bereaved oasis and fill her abysms of pain
where Humour for burial is wrapped in a shroud.
When Satire expires, Laughter mourns in elegies
When the village tale-teller falls, children croon dirges
and wander around and wonder aloud
Payo, African Canary, how did you fly to the sky
and melt as hailstone from two fingers on high?

Black Box

IAN KETEKU

In every heart is a black box
a telegraph to the great beyond
On the walls of this box is a letter
written in sunlight and vapour
a record of the granite we laid in silence
the battles fought in solitude
rustic umber drifting
It holds our fears
too mundane to be spoken
the sound of your mother's hands
and the ashes you left behind
There is a gift which time has stolen
this too the box holds with grace
The box knows
the faces worth remembering
it palms the screams in Abuja
holds tight to your beloved's tears
puddling to the brim
enough to quench the drought
for the journey to the great beyond.

   ***

In Tibet the dead are taken to a mountain
where their body is swallowed
by warm wind, molting vultures
—by anything with a mouth
The birds swirl and circle beneath clouds
their weighted bellies full of sacrificeTibetans call it the sky burial
but every funeral is a gift to the skies
a return to the mist which shaped us
our mother's lavender hands
   ***

There is only one who can read the box
transcribe the fingerprints in silk
The Creator reads the ornament's library
and weighs your intentions with grace
   For not every warrior is a martyr
it depends on the worth of the fight
but you were a man of honour, of midnight dew
and loud brilliance
   So when Allah holds your heart
and lifts up your black box
he will see it wet, and heavy, and brilliant
sunlight leaking on its skin.

Paramour of the Pen

ABRAHAM TOR

The sun peeps behind the eclipse
As dark shrouds gather in her face.

Dark angels hover like vultures
For the carrion of the human soul.

Silence! Pen maestro goes home
And silence stalks the land like puny shadows.

But the soul selects her guide!
Dark shroud and angels are no chaperones for the pen.
Hah! There is light beneath our sky
Where the pen begins a new chapter

In a diary of sparkling feats.
Adesanmi: paramour of the pen!

Flying Coffin

JAMES ONYEBỤCHI NNAJI

A golden coffin
Soaring high
At an insane speed
Suddenly explodes
In flames
Towering down
Through thick woods
With tens of thousands
Nailed
For a final travel
To the grave.

Its wings clipped
Feathers flaming
Smoke oozing
Through the burning world.
The coffin comes home
Amid Olympic of mourners.

Looking for the Dead

JAMES ONYEBỤCHI NNAJI

I plunge myself in darkness
Trembling voices resonate with tongues of fire
Questioning:
"Why do you look for the dead among the living?"
"Why not let the living bury their dead?"
Ghostly things, in deep colour of smoke, stray among us.
Every day, we invoke their benevolence
For a breath of life:
"Come forth from your realm and pacify the living!"
"Console the lonely voices weeping in the distant forest."
"Sanctify my scarred soul; the remainder
Out of the endless wails from the ashes of the last blast."
For I know that the dead is not dead.

My world caved in into emptiness
The pangs of memory engulf my whole being
Its blackness weighs heavy.
In my wet dream
I roam the road not taken
Stranded at the feet of the sacred iroko tree
Pleading for a double portion of life.

My spirit now looks for the dead
The stars have clashed across the sky
Up above, I see only the color of blood
Surging forth and brimming over.

Where do I hide my face?
I can't look at the loss of my own lodestar
For half into the world my trailing shadow died
I became a dream lost to the night
And living is only but a second death.

The Eagle Perched

MOSES OGUNLEYE

Not all songs come
With drums and dance
Not all days come
With rising of the sun

The great bird came back
In a swoop from the skies
Now without tales on its tail
No drums no dance

Oh Eagle
You are receding with a propensity
You have gone beyond our perspectives
Come back again and soar

Come like a celebrant
Come with drums and dance
Come back again and soar
Like an Eagle that you are

A Pius Flight

KENNEDY EMETULU

You peered into the Deep and saw the Hand
Quick He claimed you like a lost jewel found
In a world bereft of your magic wand
We search His Face in a Bishoftu mound

The winds howled the names of one five seven
The rocks cracked the secret to a stunned world
And we looked up to an empty heaven
Announcing in tears our query is bald

Our words are choked up in mid-sentences
Our heads heavy from the burden of thoughts
Death the grandmaster of false façades
Claims your presence but not your living guts

The highlight reel still rolling on the wire
Elijah out in your chariot of fire

Kwanza for Pius

IFESINACHI NWADIKE

Payo, in this long night of mournin'
We, the living-dead gather
Behind the wall of the realm
Where Abikus return to, sobbing along
The soft dirges of the tripod konga
Asking if the gods missed you so
Much, they had to call you home?

Dream-mare

NIDHAL CHAMI

Last night's dream
Woke her up
She retained a scream
Then spat in a cup

The last drops of water
The last traces of life
The last place to enter
At last without strife

Dried out of cold
Icy frozen words
Alas bought and sold
Alas read or heard

This is the land
The land where
The no man's land
stops to dare

This is a world
An earth, a planet
Where just a word
Is used as target

Money, they say,
"Time is money"
Whatever the way
Money is honey

She drank some water
Moistened her lips;
She pulled the drawer
It was full of clips

Like coins they glittered
But could only attach
Bits of her life, withered,
Too fragile to catch

It was just a nightmare
That she had to forget
No one with whom to share
And nothing with which to bet.

A Walk in the Graveyard

CHIMEZIRI C. OGBEDETO

I saw in this silent place
no man,
no man to hear my confession,
to soothe my mind's quest.
I heard voices, only
of lonely shrubs within
speak from withered leaves
seldom falling with faint thuds
from trees swaying in eerie wind.
Then chills threaten,
my resolve dampens
and fright nudges
to quit the mission.
No! No! No
My spirit in anger swells.
Speak graveyard amid your silence
For anger in this spirit dwells;
Are you not the place at last
each soul will come to rest?
Must you to our farmland come
to pluck a harvest in undue season?
Why visit as the ripening fruits caress
the labourer's heart...
when the barn all ready-made
for the great harvest?
Why do you in silent mockery lie,
with no heed to the sounds of the ikoro
heralding the festival dance
for the HERO of our muse?
Too early,
you plucked the ripening fruit.

Payo

BIKO AGOZINO

He studied the Holy Ghost at length,
He taught Pentecostalism to his novices,
His writings aestheticized the flowery diction,
He could speak in tongues fluently, he said.
He raised his voice against principalities,
Against the ruling dominions, he railed,
And against the powers that be; he
Never accepted them as his leaders.
He was born again and again and again!
He could possess his portions with pride,
Also could reject evil liars, in Jesus name,
And send evil schemes back to sender.
He could bind the one he called his enemy
And blunt all weapons fashioned against him;
He could cast psalms at his enemies, said he,
To make a thousand fall by his right hand
And another ten thousand by his left!
Who were the foes against whom he wailed,
'If only you, God, would slay the wicked?'
"Away from me, you who are bloodthirsty."
The Psalmist in 139 begged to be tested
And bragged for the Lord to search him
And see if there was any offensiveness:
Forgive our debts as we forgive our debtors
Love your enemies as yourself, echoed MLK,
Bless those who curse you. But why?
Because the name of your worst enemy
Could be on your very own passport.
Go and change and come again, selector,
For Iya Stool knows the meaning of
'La Luta Continua, Solidarity Forever'
Victory is Certain; for the Survivors Live.

Iku

PETER OLAMAKINDE OLAPEGBA

Silent yet so loud
Stealth yet grabbing in full glare
Hated but still the final companion
I am Iku, your ultimate owner

You fear me but must succumb to me
Rejected but celebrate when I come calling
Strong bones bow at my whims
I am Iku, the foe you must embrace

In darkness I tread boldly
In daylight caution is my friend
All souls pour libation at my feet
I am Iku, the end of all struggles

Wail or cry care I not
Blood and soul unsatisfied appetite
The bottomless pit that gulps
I am Iku, the end of your aspirations.

Your cry, my laughter
Your wail my dance
The bright sun I put to sleep
I am Iku, the dreaded darkness.

He left

AMATORITSERO EDE

                He left

                On a day when
                the sky was
              a carnivorous bowl

                                    in heaven
            the sea a thunderous
                    muddy cauldron
                              on earth

                the algae and seaweed
                    shrunken to ragged deathly
                              wisps

                the roads were
                      swollen with floodwater
                and grief

                on that day when
                    the clouds carried
                a cancer in its cotton folds

                and the tides
                    heaved and thrashed
                and broke the riverbanks

                he looked death in the eye
                    stepped on a plane
                and flew into the maelstrom

                one pius morning
                    he left
                in a hurry

Spousal Loss

PETER OLAMAKINDE OLAPEGBA

Stinging pains unrelenting
Tears for unfulfilled promises
A bilateral future eternally compromised
Yet the-left-behind bravely trudged on
Beyond the dark clouds a silver lining
A rainbow of future hope beckoning
Keeping faith for destination ever so near—

Surely, the living shall apprehend
That which the departed desired.

The Face of My Savior is the Ordinary Moment

GLORIA NWIZU

In the crumpled bible page with gum,
 I underlined Salvation

Three times.

Swallowed another piece of gum to preserve the organs.
       Chewed some groundnut and soap after.

I woke up
 As catholic as I was the day before,
Boiled

My chaplet like an egg and stirred
      Like a wheel rolled by gypsies evading
Borders by crossing them.

Said my prayers.
      Colored

The skyline with questions blue.
 Blue as the scarf that connects
The seven days.

    Jumped from the gash of the earth.

 Landed in the sink washed. Safety
Becoming under Joshua's tree.
The tiring birth

Just
      Done.

Home now sacred. Family

Given hearty second platters.
        Hope belts out the City of Lights.

The cut of the tender gum by the sharp white shell is the best thing given.

Denouement

GLORIA NWIZU

When we were at fresh height, we used to run.
Until he ran past and never returned.
Those legs. His legs. Like risen anchors.
Of them I dreamt and dreamt. And thought, focused,
What almighty stools they would make
For offerings, noble flags, minds of peace.

A Conversation between Two Young Cousins

ETHEL NGOZI OKEKE

Lolu, see my teddy
It's big...so lovely, so soft and fluffy
You'll see mine soon, Odun
When Uncle Payo takes me to the mall
Yes, he said so: he'll take me to the mall
To get me toys and lots more
You'll see mine soon
Uncle said he'll spoil me
Said he will
O, you'll see—
wait until Uncle comes back!
Oh, no! But that can't be.
Never again!
Odun, why not?
Yes, of course...
Uncle Payo said it!
Said I could have anything
Wait till he's back!
Then you'll see!
No, but the news! The news...
Didn't they tell you?
The news, what?
Uncle said it
And he'll do it! And you tell me the news
The news, what?
Sorry, they didn't tell you?
Didn't tell you—there's an air crash
And Uncle is no more!
Liar...you're such a damn liar...liar!
Uncle Payo's coming back, of course

Told you he'll take me to the mall!
You're jealous, that's why
Because I'm Uncle's best
And you're not—liar!
Uncle's coming back
You wait, he's coming back
Then I'll tell him the wicked things you say
Wait till he comes!
Don't know... But Dad said it...
It was on the news Dad and all of them were crying
Saw them all crying They said Uncle died!
That's not true! Shut up...I don't want to hear!
Wicked liar, I'm going to tell Uncle I'll tell him
But I'm serious, Lolu
It's true!
Noooooooo!
How can that be true?
Not true, not true, not true! Can never be true
You liar!
Here comes Aunty!
Aunty Lara, is it a lie?
Didn't Uncle Payo die?
And Dad and all of them were crying Aunty, tell Lolu it's true!
The truth, finally, dawned his piercing scream,
Shattered even the hearts of lions with wide-eyed disbelief
To that nightmare of March 10, 2019!
As the roof crashed on our heads
As our mountain fell
As the rope caught our elephant
As our jar split, splashing its contents
As the Darkness seized our Day brimming with promises
And his cycle was done
And the bell tolled for him, as well as for us

Sunday Flight

EMMAN USMAN SHEHU

In this ancient land of pilgrimages,
cockpit switches stir devices
alive. One flickers—March Ten, Twenty-Nineteen
and bleeps the time—Eight Thirty-Eight AM.
On another, the digital map lays out
a red-arrowed flight path –
unusual colour choice in retrospect –
from Bole to Nairobi,
as straight as this metallic crow would go.

*

A Sunday morning ensemble
like a global palette
takes in the assurance ritual,
strapped in the comfort of anticipation;
the hour of arrival
at a common destination
and the motley of engagements –
sight-seeing, reunions, meetings,
conferences or transit arrangements,
a time in the oasis of calm.

*

The new flying machine
imperiously coaxes off gravity –
nature's complex construct,
inclines towards the skies
thrusting its majestic engine.
The fascination of flying
flashes across in brief smiles.

*

Six minutes post-takeoff
an erratic vertical speed
brings the big bird down.
An unscheduled termination
South East of Addis Ababa.
Strewn aground in Bishoftu,
debris of reality
signposting life's fragility
and technology's vulnerability.

*

Bad news encircles the globe
like ribbons of calamity.
We debrief manifest of nationalities,
our shared humanity spinning hope
in anxious heartbeats.
We look beyond numbers
for factual feel of names.
We scour for unnoticed premonitions
on social media pages,
recent narratives and text messages.
We reel in scraps
of choice moments from the past
in words that despondently fail
to staunch our bleeding hearts.
We watch the news channels
spilling discomforting explanations –
like the obsession for fuel efficiency
breeding a tragic deficiency.
We hear sound bites of grief;
One says, "My heart is on fire."
Our hearts are craters
of huge losses and ache.

Departure

IVOR AGYEMAN-DUAH

I
Imperial to Global: Ibadan to Beijing and Back.
Wole Soyinka was dense with this and wandered!
White wines at table afterwards!
Before the red and food, Pius Adesanmi, the protagonist told stories.
Gory accident at the Ibadan-Lagos Highway included.
He showed evidence, the lameness of his left-hand, artificial-looking.
We listened:
voice, very satirical and with gesticulation of face and hands:
of his unimaginable survival.
'It almost claimed me.'
Not yet though.
We clinked glasses to good health.

II
Morning after.
Multitude of luggage dotted the hotel lobby space.
Departures back to our different worlds.
CODESRIA 2018 is almost close for the business of our many travels.
But the harmattan of Dakar gathered power into Christmas.
The lobby space is sightless of Adesanmi.
Soyinka came down with light luggage.
We were to gather for the airport.
We did without him.
He went there before us.
Obedient to check-in and aviation ethos.
Our destinations: Dakar-Abidjan-Accra for Adesanmi and I.
       Dakar-Abidjan-Lagos for Soyinka.

III
Abidjan transit arrival.
Over-heard the loud laugh-off behind me.
His, of course!
Apologies aloud:
'Did not want to miss the Dakar-Abidjan leg'.
Flights beckoned to him!
He responded in hurry!!
Always!!!
To duty of scholarship and friendship.
Dakar-Abidjan-Accra was west coast.
Flight ET 302– Addis Ababa- Nairobi was east coast;
a human cargo, Boeing 737- a minaret-like sphinx of new technology.
Still, he fell on the soil of the continent.
One he taught to other worlds.
In destined time and place, it was still fateful.
No ordinary beckon.
Death!
Inclement ways and by-ways!!

The Count

UTHPALA DISHANI SENARATNE

On a red carpet of blood
lay a multitude of young men and women.
What do their half-decayed bodies
smell like: victory or defeat?

Roughly, the wind blows
asking them to
haunt their loved ones,
who
tremble
in a deadly
breeze.

Gulping down rice and curry
many watch the nightly news.
"How many terrorists have been killed?
Fifty-eight.
How many army fellows have been killed?
Eight."

How nice!
How patriotic!
They go to sleep.

Rude Shock

OLAJIDE SALAWU

Once I knew you are no longer
returning and buzzards don't play
dead except they lose their wings,
each morning my grief comes anew
like a dew misting on the jungle
face of my country.

I burn these white candles
to see where your body may be in this
darkness, and in this deadening silence
I call you back to bring me sun to see
which part of my body my country is eating today.

But my country is no longer
eating me; it is eating your name
in its mouth like long-lost lovers
in a strange prodigal embrace.

Saturday 12:56

LUDWIDZI M. K. MAINZA

"If I take the wings of the morning,
And dwell in the uttermost parts of the sea,
Even there Your hand shall lead me,
And Your right hand shall hold me…"
And steady me
As I walk on water,
And marvel at the beauty,
The beauty of the sea.

Nigeria wails tonight,
All eyes glued to their televisions.
Which poet will write my eulogy?
Who will dare sing my song?
How many men
Will pay tribute to the man, Pius Adesanmi?

Lay your pretty flowers here
Next to the Wayfarer,
Make sure they are 157
For I do not walk alone.

On Saturday at 12:56,
An angel came to me,
But I think I forgot all that he said
Except for the words of Psalm 139
Which I shared with you,
Knowing it was my last goodbye.

Daughter

LUDWIDZI M. K. MAINZA

Mama says you're gone.
The computer screen is on.
Mama says you fell from the sky.
Is that why she cried all night?

Faceless shadows softly convey their
Deepest sympathies,
Condolences
And "sorry for your loss"
While the solemn choir sings on.

But none of that will bring you back
Or comfort my aching heart
Because only your warm hugs
And playful kisses
Can mend my breaking heart.

Tough Love

NNOROM AZUONYE

Many words written. Many words spoken.
Urgently. Fearlessly. Mercilessly. You get
only one lifetime to touch many lives in their times.
With a sword cut from tears of a bleeding nation
you snatched the songbook of eggshells
from hesitant hands under the iroko and hid it
in the heartwood where cowards will never find it.

You burst forth unto our digital village square;
a town crier walking without shoes on burning coal,
like The Baptist in a connected wilderness;

Change—flee mediocrity—denounce corruption—
or be buried with it...

Many words written. Many words spoken.
Many feathers ruffled. Many stews of anger cooked.
Yet we loved you more than we could fathom.
and sparred with you in this cacophonic arena;
flexing words, painting shades of truth.

Fighting with the kin this way looked good on you
and we wanted more. We needed more...

...but you flew away. You flew away...for good.

This friendship and our conversations were supposed
to endure until days of no teeth and no eyes come;
our palm wine cups seen with palms of our hands
as we reminisce about the years, we battled to save our country
armed only with weapons made from words and hearts...
but we did not factor into these thoughts, life and its tricks,
or that our battleground is built with ceramic bricks.

In the Midst of it All, I am…

ANUSHYA RAMAKRISHNA

I am from the scorching sun,
beating down on people undone.
I am from the dried- up fields,
barren from the drought exposed yields.
I am from the tears of anger,
at life's unfair ways, hopelessness turned to rancor.
I am from the wails of sorrow,
as souls float away, robbed of a tomorrow.
I am from the hunger,
that on a noose hung her.
I am from the stillborn child,
a life denied.
I am from the orphaned one
whose life saw no sun.

Through this darkness within me shines a light.

I am the ray of sun,
that draws from brown colors of green, life has won.
I am the rain,
that washes away life's pain.
I am the tears of joy,
puppy in hand, coursing down the cheeks of the little boy.
I am the battle against strife,
victory by life.
I am the dissipated hunger,
in both older and younger.
I am the newborn wail,
from the bundle of joy, arms flail.
I am the cautious acceptance
of a stolen family and love, one giving into dependence.

In the midst of all the ugly,

within me grows the beautiful,
and there is hope for the world
because of that beautiful in me.

Haiku – Ai-Ku (Immortality)

ADESANYA ADEWALE ADESHINA

Dust to dust
Ashes to ashes before
The Phoenix lifted!

He Rose

ADESANYA ADEWALE ADESHINA

Sunset at dawn
In order to birth
A new horizon
Paradise lost
For the high prospects
Of gaining heaven
He-Rose!

A Singing Bird

ADESANYA ADEWALE ADESHINA

There was once a young skylark from Africa
Who flew across the Atlantic to sing an opera
The Crown and the Rosary
Penned praises to his poetry
Before the great poet awoke from his siesta!

Arrivant

AKUA LEZLI HOPE

Overthrow this empire of reason
the dominance of intellect over love
fact over truth, data subsumes knowledge
misconstruing science to leave
things out

Beginning will be found in the end
this world is an old mind,
a dreaming mind, storytelling mind
We must relocate eternity.

In New York, standing on a street corner,
we can see stars, hear part
of their great song, the mystery inside
trying to reveal itself

Old woman in mystic blue cave
diligently weaves for eons
forest-gathered porcupine quills
into a singing garment

She must pause to stir
the pot of all the seeds
and plants of the world
when she rises to mix this soup
her waiting grey dog
pulls a loose thread,
unravels the raiment
She beholds the mess,
repairs and starts to weave again

We're in Scheherezade times
telling a stirring story each incensed night
to keep ourselves alive tomorrow

She weaves the broken, bitter king
back into himself, into the world
saving herself and all her sisters
using the web of ancient stories
as my grandmother did, applying
spider webs to heal
my father's wounds, scarless

We must join in reweaving
We are Isis gathering, freeform crocheting
scattered, broken pieces of Osiris

Near us, something small asks to be saved
not too heavy to carry, it becomes
a great fuel that survives
when the over culture collapses

Noah minds, carry your own
little fish of self, smaller than small inside
tied to the bigger than big, dreaming

Power of the mustard seed:
parables older than books
lore is our heart's learning
law was made when we forgot

Why can't we see god anymore?
because we don't bend low enough

We are being called by the little
fish to save the world
in the little fish that Manu saved was Vishnu

Stories formed primordial thought
in our old mind. Touch beginnings again,
return to paradise, handle the paradox
of being alive at the end of the beginning

This has all happened before:
Take the little thing talking to you
and carry it as far as you can

you will bump into other people
carrying what they can
and our world will be remade.

EarthWork Sestina

AKUA LEZLI HOPE

the man who left water in the desert
was charged for littering. He had found
a 14 year-old girl dead from illness and want,
having sent her brother on. His simple solution
to save lives. Like that college guy who bid
without money to save wilderness lands

faces prosecution for saving those lands
Who wants children left dying in the desert?
Being the people we seek, we should bid
to save our air, our land. So much is found
in quiet places, respite, healing, a solution
to what ails us, to ease our gnawing want

which has so outstripped our needs. We want
and with technology, take from other lands
then decree what may be a solution
but shreds hilltops, turns grassland to desert
steals water from wherever it may be found
ignoring native needs, enslaved to the highest bid

We distract ourselves as we bid
on frail lotteries which do not ease deep want
paying failed banks more. Our losses are found
in coal mountain-slides, in strip-mined lands
filling green valleys with sludge, wrecking fragile desert
increasing unmet debts with a dire solution

Past wisdom reimagined holds the solution
what occurs clean, harnessed, is the best bid
collect sun, gather wind, regreen the desert
new laws may constrain this issue of want
yet wars rage for control of resource-rich lands
where minerals, metals and oil are found

Here in this retrograde cross, magic is found
numerological formulations hold a solution
We've fought, bled and died to save our lands
from exploitation, alien auctions. Stop the bid
rewarding a powerful few despite what many want
How long does it take to evolve? We can't desert

this shining blue anomaly is humanity's best bid
solutions wait within. Protect from overreaching want,
this sphere, save all lands from rainforest to desert.

Animalia, Chordata, Mammalia, Proboscidea

AKUA LEZLI HOPE

Once you were millions
roaming every continent
except Australia and Antarctica
favoring a side: right or left tusked
replacing teeth like a conveyor belt
the new shoving the old forward
creating sunscreen with mud wallow masks
tiptoeing on a cushion that swells under pressure
or shrinks as you lift the foot
freeing you from any sticky situation

You walk or run
Sailwide ears wing you
flap and cool your blood
Efficient in herbivorous inefficiency
16 hours a day you work to feed your mass
ripping leaves, chewing grass
your undigested spent fuels others
clears space for new growth
your coveted tusks debark trees
dig for salt, roots, water, providing for more

Your nose lip arm hears as well as caresses,
breathes as well as showers,
100,000 muscles for your snorkel hose hand
carry water to your mouth, lift logs

You are small grey mountains with a bigger brain
and much to say through subsonic rumbling
infrasound traveling through the ground
further than that dazzling

trumpet through the air,
things humans cannot hear

Mothers, daughters, sisters, aunts
cousins, all for all and many to care
for babies, long carried
within, welcomed upon arrival,
long protected, long taught
peace, play, light, love, family
our appetite for your tooth tool has
your elders dying too soon
leaving few teachers
for your young.

Poem of Relief: When Your Sadness is Alive

KENNEDY HUSSEIN ALIU

When your sadness is alive
Hold its head down between
The tight-grips of your thighs
Pick up your razor blade,
Begin to shave its hair barren.

When your sadness is alive
Lend your grandmother's cutlass
Bless it with her amulets
Grab it by its neck—slaughter it.

When your sadness is alive
Stab it. Take the dagger your father
hunts with—Pierce the chest
until you see the crimson red
spill on your cold hands
Do not be afraid
It is trophy for torment.

When your sadness is dead
Don on your black abaya
lay it silently in the coffin
prepare its burial
curse it to the grave
to death
to earth

If I Seek

KENNEDY HUSSEIN ALIU

If I seek validation
validate me. Tar and rinse me,
in your hallelujahs
Let the Jericho's, built for heart
Plummet.

Absolve me of all ancestral guilt.
My oracle demands worship
Worship me.
When I expose my ugly divinities,
As reluctant, as it seems,
validate me.
For in this realm
beggars can be choosers.
If I seek Acceptance
accept me.
I am the cracked toothed
prodigal omen born into destitution.
The masquerade that dances
with bangles latched to my ankles.
I am the prisoner of profane spaces
and vain glories
cursed with a distant destiny.
accept me.
For in this realm
beggars can be choosers.

If I seek healing
heal me.
Cast me naked, pour unto me,
your oils of unholy liberations
Bathe me,
In words—of extinct languages

only your griot grandmother remembers.
Be patient with her.
As with every cough, sneeze,
and snuff,
Tell me these words.

If I seek conformity
Kill me.
Make mounds of my rotten carcass
Like the fig tree,
O son of Palestine, curse me barren.
For I have mirrored death.
Impale my body on horns of the oryx
Spill my blood,
That it may sanctify the land
Bury me
In memory, as the "one who seeked."

When You Ask me About my Teacher

KENNEDY HUSSEIN ALIU AND LEYDA JOCELYN ESTRADA ARELLANO

When you ask me about my teacher,
I tell you I sing sweet palm-wine melodies of his name.
Professor Pius Adebola Adesanmi,
you stood as tall as the sagole baobab tree
Muri Kunguluwa; 'the tree that roared'—that yelled.
Unabashed by its branches.
digging and connecting ancestral knowledges
That made ripples at home and the diaspora

When you ask me about my teacher,
I tell you about his voice, and how it rested like tattoos on
our skin. His words bled culture
Creating spirited revolutions that broke the confines of our minds.
Reminding us that he was the Abiku
The profane child, yet a man, who transcended the humane
And encompass all that was divine.

When you ask me about my teacher,
I tell you about how I danced as I listened to the songs
He played on the umbilical cords of Mother Africa
And how he demanded the children of the continent to listen.
They rarely listen.
But if they did, they would hear his words about how our destinies
Were born to rise like the yeast in bofrot, akara, mandazi, mikate, puff-puff.

When you ask about my teacher,
I tell you about loss.

When he was here,
The wooden door glimmered with all the colours
Created by God
Intricate carved designs
Deep enough for sea creatures to swim in
Every dip mesmerizing
Exciting

When you ask about my teacher,
Now, I tell you that the door is gray
There are no designs
Just a single deep hollow
Colors melted onto the ground
Leaving a distraught pattern
I scrape it everyday
Knees chafed by prolonged kneeling
Rag burning my palms
But it never goes away
Just seeps further into the floor
Permanent.

The Eagle is not the Quills and Talons

OLUMIDE OLANIYAN

The sky beckons the bald eagle to ascend
To espy new rocks and forests for the eaglets' abode
Where sparrows and pigeons will not gamble
As wonted, she storms against the gales unfazed
Piercing the skies, navigating cliffs, trumping seas
Near the horn of Africa – on the wings of the morn
Hurtling in her quotidian mission to conquest
It's an hour the ether is enmeshed in idolatry
The eagle, the unconcerned ether plunks into a firestorm
Blazing her quills, her talons, her beak and viscera –
A vain try to eclipse a life force

Alas, the eagle is not the quills or the talons
She is not the beak, the wings or the innards
She is a pious whip lacerating mediocre rulers
A force making frail voices bark back at oppressors
A taste of wit, wisdom and triumph in thorny tussles
She is a morn that avows human transience and frailty.

without a farewell

NDUKA OTIONO

where do we go from here
after 47 moonshines and star-lit nights?

where do we go from here, wayfarer,
after the winged tube forgot to kiss the sky god,

staggered like Klint da drunk
and lunged into Bishoftu's mass grave?

where do we go from here, towncrier
after the calabashes of our dreams broke

mid air like Baba Elemu's wine cask, spilled
blood as libations, reddened the earth

and scorched the brambles on their Sunday
morning worship in Haile Selassie's country.

we were not stingy with prayers to ancestors
we were not forgetful, when we missed

saying goodbye on the eve of departures
sharing the secrets of our burdened lives.

did the guardian spirits abdicate the altar
when our eyes were watching God?

do they know where we go from here, homeros of Isanlu,
as your musings face me, and I book you, reading

diaries of everyday errors in the rendering on Facebook
as Brodsky hums: "The grave will render all alike,"

and Walcott, filled with St Lucia pride, sights the old man
coming through the glass and queries: "who are you?

"Do you think Time makes exceptions, do you think
Death mutters, 'Maybe I'll skip this one'?"

we searched for you through the manifest rubbles
but death, dark like your skin, failed to skip you one more time,

and Bàbá Alábẹ's magic could not chain the secret door to Asaro's
Higherworld to keep you a prisoner of war amongst us earthlings.

and so, here we are, plaiting wreaths for you,
vagrant of 47 moonshines and star-lit nights,

farewell, farewell, fare the well, troubadour, and all
you soul brothers who left midlife without a farewell.

After the Funeral

NDUKA OTIONO

yesterday, Ottawa was draped
with glorious sunlight
today, Ottawa is drenched
in somber rain

across the city this Sunday morn'
the wind harasses trees
and leaves falling leaves
across lawns and roads

it's Fall and nature celebrates the arrival
of an important guest and i wonder
what conversation the sky and the soil
had overnight after we left the cemetery—

if you listen, you'd hear Nature speak
of the eternal cycle: life and death.

(October 27, 2019)

Fugitives from the Violence of Truth

EFE PAUL-AZINO

We inhabit the singer's demons
Stumble through his traumas
from kitchen to bathroom to bed

The city is heavy with the smell
of the day's failures. Tired engines
grumble into the ears of the window.

I have come to bury my memories
in the fires where you seek yours,
fugitive from the violence of truth.

The silence of my children has hatched
resentment and travelled from the future
to haunt me. I plunge my head in your

laughter and breathe. The singer wonders
if he'll end up in prison like Vybez Kartel or dead.
His visions hang over our naked bodies in autotune, dizzy with promise,

outside the world breaks another,
an airplane buries itself in Ethiopian earth, yields a lamentation,
an elephant dies but his dreams thunder through the earth,

rallying the battle-weary forces of truth,
teasing language from the bleeding jaws of hate,
death is on the bus, death is in the throat of the faithful collecting their prayers,

death is in the school yard, death gets home before the kids
death is in the rotting courage of the clergy, death is in the

politician's greed
death is in our love, hanging unlawful between our breaths.

Just but a Journey

SAM DENNIS OTIENO

Of flights and farewells,
Plans and passions,
Paths and places,
Pause...
It's all but a journey.

Of quests and questions,
Classrooms and conferences,
Countries and continents,
Skies and soils,
Silence...
It's all but a journey.

Of lectures and laughter,
Discourses and debates,
Divergences and convergences,
Dream...
It's all but a journey.

On Africa you spoke,
For Africa you dreamt,
With Africa you rest,
Son of our soil,
We shall reap from your toil,
For this all, is just but a journey.

PART II
REQUIEMS

Elegy for Pius

HELON HABILA

That's how we planned it—

Because we did not feel at home at home
We travelled the world

Flushed out of our little crannies by the spring rain
That promised cleansing and renewal

We left the streets of Lagos and landed breathless on foreign shores
And despite being the wrong color,
Speaking the wrong accent, naija no de carry last

Homeless, we carried home in our hearts —
We wrote songs of longing, songs for Zion, songs of return

We would win accolades, break records, storm citadels
And bring home the laurels—
We would return in time to stitch the broken fabric of our land,

That was the plan, Pius

But time is a shapeshifter, turning days to months, months to years
Black hair turns gray turns bald

That is not how we planned it, to become homeless in this world,
Visitors on the streets of Lagos; eternally departing and returning

Yet defiant we glow, against the odds we twinkle,
Distant stars in distant firmaments, shining, defiantly shining, even as time
And gravity pluck us out of our milky ways and ivory towers.

This Exodus Has Birthed a Song

ECHEZONACHUKWU NDUKA

On that morning of cracking mirrors,
wings folded midway and slammed the earth
in disbelief. Who paved this sudden new path for the wayfarer?
The right hand of God or the left hand of man?
Why did the bell toll at the forty-seventh count?
Does this dream of coming and going sting the most at odd numbers?
What do we do with tears that flow without permission, without stopping
for refills at memory stations?

Here comes a time when poems must witness a new resurrection.
Read out aloud for this soul whose laughter is thunder.
Tears are drenching mourners, threatening to sink this ship of letters.
But we know that words don't sink. They don't fly and crash.
You sprouted and grew in the hearts of many, bearing a torch
for clarity of thoughts.
See now how this exodus has birthed a song, a breathing ash
redreaming the world nonstop.

where to find you: a requiem

ECHEZONACHUKWU NDUKA

not at the crash site in Bishoftu where
pools of tears and blood dried for a million questions
not in the tones of a lone twin-gong
struck after morning libations
not on the anthill paths of Isanlu
where red earth crumbles in defeat
not in the hushed voices of scholars arguing
for silence as framework for departure theories
not on the highways of Ottawa where snowflakes
assert their rights as citizens without borders

did heaven build a new classroom in a hurry?
did angels and ancestors ask for a new teacher?

you, a four-lobbed kola breaking into tongues
of home and faraway lands
you, a library weighing tons of pounds
yet moving weightless with wit into ears
is there a new lingo formed in praise of your arrival?

we turn again those pages where your voice resonates
to thousands for whom your truths endure
we turn to pathways now clear because you, wayfarer,
dared to walk ahead
we turn to reprimands to rusty crowns for whom shame
is the new grace
we turn again to memories—for there's no place
for death in its firmament.

Blown

RICHARD INYA

We are seeds in a winnower's tray
Death makes chaff of our being
Life's covering is torn asunder
Falling off with each breath

The breeze of death is tempestuous
We drop with each fleeting moment
Vanishing like darkness that strays
Into the bold brilliant arms of light

Soulful eyes hold tales, and the heart
Is an unoccupied pew in a cathedral
Repulsing the liturgy with silence
Tears sear paths on forlorn cheeks

Death ambushes at life's trajectory
Pointing the flight of garlanded necks
Towards the house of mourning
Festive songs make way for requiem

Life is a ride on the brow of fate
The careful don't even land their sail
The dance of a bird and stormy wind
Ends in orgasmic convulsion in the mud

words melt in his mouth

PETER MIDGLEY

words melt in his throat, emerge dark as honey.
the night's clamminess ushers in the rattletrap dance of skeletons
against the horizon. they are legion, like the sands of the sea
and the skulls in the sand
the sailors the explorers the wanderers
the prisoners of this land.
they are legion. they are silent.

they have died in multiple ways,
each death a parting and a return.
who knows from whence they came.
what is departure? what is return?

taste the earth—
no, taste the earth,
go down on your hands and knees
dig down below the browned hide
to where the desert sand throbs a darkened red.
fill your fingernails with this soil, let it sink again black as honey,
this ink of my body, into the blotted desert.

taste the earth.
smell it.
feel it.
feel its textures and its joys
weeping to the surface
like water: the sorrow
the heartache
the bones of the ancestors
drying in poisoned wells.
taste this earth and feel its pain.

taste the earth
blotted with the ink of many bodies.

Requiem for the Fallen / Mogaka o ole

LEBOGANG DISELE

Can there be too many poems for those gone too soon?
Can there be enough songs to remind us of the fragility of life?
Can we write too much about death, about loss?
Would it be enough?

I think about you all, sitting there.
Looking forward to the promise of tomorrow.
Were you thinking about your seat?
Looking around, hoping for an empty spot to escape to?
Or were you looking out the window?
Trying to catch a final glimpse of the city?
Perhaps you were sending a text,
A reminder of your arrival,
Anticipating your reunion.
I think about you all,
Faces I never met, faces I will never meet, faces I may have never met.
But faces gone too soon.

I think of you, left behind
I can feel your heart sinking into your stomach, as you hear the news.
You know.
I can hear the ringing in your ears before silence engulfs you, and everything stops
I can hear your heart beating,
Racing in denial, trying to jump out of your chest.
Trying to stop the unbearable pain washing over your body.
"This can't be happening!" you scream in disbelief.
Why you? Why him? Why her? Why…
What can we do for you?

We think of you,
Those of us who pray, pray for you
We write poems and sing songs for you,
Wishing your life better for fear of our own helplessness.
Will it ever be enough?

Mogaka o ole

(Setswana: Translation)

Heelang batho!
Ke utlwang?!
Pelesa e ole!
Pelesa e e gogang kwa pele e sa gatelelwa!

Kana ke raya Pius,
Yole wa ga Adesanmi!

A leka go re gogela ka fa metsing aa didimetsing,
A leka go re bontsha mafulo a a matalana.
A leka go re bontsha gore golo ha, lesaka le phunyegile.
A leka go re raya a re re age lesaka sesha.
Sa le a re emetse ka dinao, mme re palelwa ke go mo utlwa.
   O re lekile ka maretshwa otlhe.
O kgalemile jaaka mogolo a tshwere ngwana wa seganana,
A neneketsa jaaka moeti a kopa dilalelo,
A re tshegisa ka metlae a re gongwe re tlaa lemoga fa leso legolo e le ditshego.
Ke raa!

A mo ke gone mo go tweng go bonwa ke Modimo?
Ga se gore gongwe RraMasedi o re lemogile?
A bona go tshwanela gore a bitse morongwa wa gagwe?
A mmiletse gae, kwa mahulong a matalana ka rona re ga re a kgatlhegele?

Re tlaa reng, fa e se go ikgomotsa ka gore kwa o teng o ikhuditse?

Ba a ba rutileng ba tlaa tsweledisa tema ya gagwe,
Ba ba neng ba sa mo itse ba tlaa mmona ka ditiro tsa gagwe.

To Our Hero: Rest in Peace

LEBOGANG DISELE

Mournful wailing pierces the horizon,
Life comes to a standstill
As our collective world quakes
At the fall of a giant.

Pius Adesanmi.
Son. Husband. Father. Friend. Teacher. Writer.
He who has spent his life standing up for Africa,
Trying to show us our light,
Trying to move us to (re) claim our power,
Trying to pull us out of our plight.
Pushing against the tide of our ignorance,
Always smiling,
Always inspired,
His eyes shining bright,
Never losing hope in our potential.

Did God decide to call you home,
To give you rest?
What is left but to comfort ourselves
With the hope that you are in a better place,
To tell ourselves that your students will continue your work,
That your books will spread your wisdom,
And through your writing your ideas will live on?
What is left but to wish you a peaceful rest?

Goodbye, Pius.
Son. Husband. Father. Friend. Teacher. Writer.
Warrior for freedom.
May your soul rest in peace.

What Shall We Do to Death?

WINLADE ISRAEL

What shall we do to a death
That creeps into a home,
Eats up its pillars
And leaves elegies as songs?

How on earth shall we banish death
That walks into a palace,
Claims the throne-owner
And leaves requiem to eulogise
The departed queen's crown?

How do we treat the death
That visited our land
To beat the drum of loss
And caused oasis of tears on our cheeks?

Death is a distant friend
A close enemy
He heals pain and causes tears
Distance defines his identity

A Star Just Fell

WINLADE ISRAEL

The sun is dark
The moon is red
Blood spilled from the sky
And curtain of dirge covered the sun
The larks raise the dirge
Tears spill from men's face
A star has fallen before dusk
Death has eaten one more brain in service
Rest on Pius

Requiem

PETER AKINLABI

Words treat you kindly
Even now when you wait in incompletion
Ecstasies of utterance buoy you aloft

It's your own ritual tool-kit, lyre and language
And a most apprehensive eye, primed
To rustle in ancient reprises or new chorales.

Death is colonisation
Where the arcs of the body must shift to dark.
And you knew that vale, its thrall, its invasion.

Your spirit, singed in dreams, etched its uneasiness
On a space of blue, curated degrees of distance,
And sent hallowed memos out as cure and worldview

You knew that vale; you knew you could not finish your reading
You knew from how sad the flesh had become
You knew by the slow, liturgical progression of your mother's call,

She, a supplicant, traversing worlds for repossession–
Ero aiye! ero orun! E ma pa omode yi,
E f'ori omode yi bun mi o!

But the arcs of the body must shift to the dark
For the dart of mistletoes had moved
From hand to hand

Requiem for Pius

RASAQ MALIK GBOLAHAN

What remains is a dirge woven
by a bird searching for a home
where home is a war-torn land,
a field of unclaimed bodies, a diary
of names lost to the wind of time.
What remains is no longer a country
of songs, but a camp
where we wake up daily to ask
if freedom is the chain that bears
the blood of black bodies ferried
across the middle passage to the newland.
What remains after your exit is a broken door,
a room full of people cursing your country
and its leaders, a house full of mourners
reciting your name, stretching
their hands to reach you in places
where the light of the world can no longer
reach. Pius, now that the sky is bereft of stars
tonight, your homeland becomes a widow howling
like a caged bird, a child craving love where love
is an abyss. We miss your voice in the cathedral
of words. We search for solace in your words that
bear the aches of generations, in your words that
remind us that even in your absence we shall remember
you the way a hero is remembered after his departure,
the way a bard is remembered after his death.

Wayfarer

RASAQ MALIK GBOLAHAN

In the end we will remember those
who have gone beyond us, those whose
names linger in the air of a country where
bombs reduce everywhere to a mass grave
for people who pledge to serve. In the end
we will remember our loved ones, and tears
will descend through our faces as we watch
time leave, our dreams becoming trapped by
cobwebs that blanket the corners of houses
where the dead are forgotten, where the dead
are voices unfamiliar to the world.
In the end we will remember the dead,
the moribund, and those who are about to
die in places unknown to us, places where
home is a stone that bears the names of the dead,
places where their graves become unidentified,
their graves unadorned with flowers, as nothing
survives after the death of a beloved.

Twirling the Beads of Grief...

TADE AINA

I was never taught how to make grief public,
I held my pain deep within, twirling and stringing them
In beads of prayers that I tell in numb concentration,
Shedding tears in the solitude of the depths of my wounds.
So, I hold the pains of unwanted departures, cruel stabs,
Uninvited breaks, heartbreaking resolutions of this
Primordial expulsion from Paradise's rest and peace.
From the time the forbidden fruit from the Tree of Life we stole,
By sweat, blood and tears, condemnation to bondage labor
In perennial fatigue, desire and toil we have lived.
We have forever turned vain voyagers of futile life-seas
Sailing in crafts of vanity piled upon insane inanities and futilities
We have since learned to salve sorrow, pain and loss
With natural and artificial highs invented and discovered
Desperate to reclaim the often-fleeting moments of joy,
Happiness, hope, relief and redemption that come and go,
Slack beads on tired withered waists of our maiden selves doing
Dances of sorrow and pain that remain pain and sorrow, stirring in
Now and then, joy and happiness, mere fleeting moments we taste
Swinging along in contrived fulfillment, a mirage calling the lonely wanderer
Trumpeting the bittersweet verses of our perpetual commission
To this human condition, a story Payo often told in beads of verses,
Lived in swirls of creative moons, but a nut our squirrel-selves have yet to crack.

Say me Rebellion

KINGSLEY L. MADUEKE

Keep your stories of how presidents' sons become presidents
and that shabby saying of children of merchants filling the shoes of their forebears.
Keep those.

Give me fiery tales.

Legends of how urchins of the downtrodden rise
how the girl from the backstreet took the city
and the scions of the wretched shake power.

Tell me of hardheaded commitment
the obstinacy in dedication of Yaa Asantewa
that uncommon streak that binds the doer to that which must be done.

Indulge my deepest sentiments with accounts of fire and sweat
where flames and more flames consume the heart
to bake muscles with quickness and poise.

Whisper into my restless soul the fury that stretches faith into action
and forges hope into confidence verging on the virtue of arrogance
I don't want your peace, give it to your poor.

Away with pity from my ears, be far gone
tell me not about the beggar and the clinging of coins
but of his Sun that must rise from dirt and raise a fist.

Tell me of the beating but not the retreat from Rawson's bluff
now, say nothing of those quiet dreams as we lay in the bosom of love
acquaint me with our rage, this bare-chested valour in the face of *Duc du Maine*.

>Endear me with a saga from the flaming wooded coasts where serpent eagles dare

> here, the flight is swift and the plunge steep
> screech at me from Iroko whose roots quake Gorée
> Island and divides the Aethiopian sea.

So, we must pass.

Tell me not the lies of traditions and cultures of deceptions
of kings of queens and princes and their princesses
inherited privileges and all the corruption of history.

No.

Knock me on the head, knock me cold
Say me a tale of rebellion
this is what my soul must hear.

When this Calabash Breaks

KINGSLEY L. MADUEKE

Our mothers will crouch in UNHCR-marked hovels
humming a requiem in different tongues.
Bald sunbirds, jarring and curling in ashes
But there shan't be the throaty male.
Only hollow echoes of metal, sulfur and passions.

When the calabash breaks and I sleep
I will remember my neighbour became a hound, a class cannibal.
And chased me down the twisted lanes of poverty
There we used to greet and live in worry but smiling.
I will try not to forget, I ate back and didn't wait for the gods.

When the calabash breaks and I sleep
The green-white-green rainbow that stopped the storm would lie in shreds.
No more a coverlet for these naked sisters defiled atop beds of rubbles
Yesterday's cradles of softness now chattels for the forlorn vagabond.
Death's gifted artist who sculpts the Savanah with the chisel of fear.

When the calabash breaks and I sleep
I'll be reminded that we tried as children, yes we tried even when we cried.
One time we even played and held hands and ran the fields on our toes
Who is not to know that we believed against all signs.
And so many dirty nights we spent paying for this clean faith.

When the calabash breaks and I sleep

The managers would have fled on bicycles to London.
To guest the open arms of the West and sip her Crystal
While merchant vultures circle and blur the horizon at home
In a rehearsal of hurling supplies, filling the purse and retreating mid-air.

When the calabash breaks and I sleep
And all is dust and memory and paneled cloakrooms of the Hague
When the calabash breaks and I sleep
My bones will stir on the burnt earth and ask yours.
What is Calabash?

Requiem for the Wayfarer

ADESINA AJALA

Why do you cut your light off
before dusk
To make us grope in the moonless night?

The wayfarer has blown his guiding light out
The path ahead looks map less; dim & blurry.

Why do you put dots
in the place of comma
in the sentence of a country
you wrote so much about
To make these conversations
break into unending ellipses?

The wayfarer has blown his guiding light out
The path ahead looks map less; dim & blurry.

Who stops the solemn summon
& feeds the mouth of the town crier
with threnodies of silences?
Who breaks his gong & muffles his bell
in the middle of an urgency?

The wayfarer has blown his guiding light out
The path ahead looks map less; dim & blurry.

Tonight, we gather for
procession to Bishoftu
We carry our ached necks
on our weary bodies
& stab the pains in our souls
We shall chant the words of the wayfarer
Till its embers re-burn like a phoenix
& singe this night that drapes our land.

Song of Sorrow

SOJI COLE

Shrieking sounds of pain startle our ears
Reflections starring close at us
How shall we sing a song for the unborn
When life slips out of the new-born?

Lo, the song of sorrow is written in a verse of beatitudes.

A great confusion is here over us!
As one throws the slaughtered goat into the shrine to appease the gods
And another pulls it out and roasts the corpse to appease the stomach—
Oh, now the hummingbird has gone home to roost!

And the song of sorrow has become a new anthem.

The raindrops have begun to patter on our heads
Even thunderstorms threaten our night
Noise and darkness enrapture our being
We cannot hear the call from our mother

Because the song of sorrow has shattered our nights.

Planting Season

ANOTE AJELUOROU

(for Pius Adesanmi, Bisi Silver & Okwui Enwezor)
March 16, 2019

Like yam seedlings
we planted our heroes
with fecund intellect and grace
into gluttonous mother-earth
with such rare care and tenderness.
then we feasted the whole town,
family, friends and foes, as never before;
we slaughtered seven fattened cows
and many goats and food and food
wine and ogogoro flowed
and the incontinent drowned
in the ocean of booze
and the egbaudu boomed
in the seven-day feast
and earth and heaven trembled
to booming canons
and the ancestors nodded
at the royal send-forth of our worthies
fallen Irokos in the prime of life

But alas, that was all there was
to our planting season

Our yams did not sprout to take the stakes
they remain trapped
in the bowels of greedy mother-earth
and our insides are filled
with the hollowness of loss

And time crawled by and we knew
the finality of death

and we sought healing
in meaningless chores
to fill voids of the aching heart.

For Our Departed Bard

MARIA AJIMA

Our bard, suddenly called up
For higher mission,
Has become a star of the firmaments.
Our bard departed too soon,
When we least dreamed.
Our bard flew home
In chariots of fire.

He leaped out of his mama's womb,
Like an eager panther,
Panting for justice in the world.
He was sent by the gods
To traverse the paths of the inquirer.
He came, he saw
The stinking cesspool,
Into which humanity had been thrown
By the powerful ones
But he refused to dine with them.
With words piercing like swords
He strung the words together,
Words we found hard to formulate
Even though our hearts burned with them,
For we were too dazed by their deeds.

He felt the pulse of Mother Africa
He stood on the battle lines for us
He called them out for us
And put on the gauntlet of words
And dared them do the right.
He was the voice of the people
With that impish grin that captured our hearts.
He reached out to all from coast to hinterland,
The native son schooled in native ways.

He came, fully purified,
Holding the spear of Chaka in his right hand,
And garbed in dotted skins of the leopard.
On the ultimate mission on that fateful day
He declared to the world to listen—
Clothed with the garbs of the morning wings,
The Lord's right hand led him
Joining forces with the African elite commando,
They went as a pantheon
In a blaze of fury, they lifted the veil
From the chicken's butt
To save a generation
That would have gone down
Under capitalist claws of greed.
Unbelievable whispers crowded the clouds,
P Ps Pi Piu Ps Ps Piu Ps Ps Ps
Till...rising to a crescendo,
The whole earth became stricken with grief,
For a bard departed too soon.

Memory of Tear

JOSHUA AGBO

The news gonged our skull bone
The sun stood still
The world buried its face
In dark grief on a Sunday morning
As fragments of the one
Who taught us a good spring of life
Who taught us to reject mental slavery
Were buried without a grave
We became edgy
Cursing death under our breath
For taking one of our finest
Without our permission
In anguish, we gazed up
To the ancient altar of hope
Hoping to see him again
Since he was born of life, more than of womb
His death has taught us
Not to mourn the way the old ones mourn
But to take sorrows in life
And forge into a strong monument
In the fire of our vision
With the currents of memory
That run deep in our hearts
And to conclude
That death is the only harvest of God.

Why?

MARGARET WAIRIMU WAWERU

You said you were stronger
You said you would be okay
You even promised to come home
So why did you die?
Why am I seeing the hearse in our home?
Why are all the people attending your interment?

You said you felt better
Said that you didn't need more morphine
Assured me that the trial medicine
Was giving great results
You said that the migraines were gone
So then why did you die?

You said your legs were getting stronger
That you would be up and walking in no time
That that bed wasn't going to confine you anymore
So, tell me why are you in the Afterlife?

You said you remembered
Your grandmaster chess moves
You joked that you would be fool mating me in few weeks time
So, tell me baby
Why can't I wake you up?

You told me to wipe my tears
You told me to be strong
You told me to wait for you
I remember you telling me
I will force you to visit all my favourite spots*
Why didn't you keep your word?

You told me to prepare your room
You gave me strict orders to wash your favourite tango duvet

You told me to decorate your room with glowing stars
So, princess
Why did you leave me?

Why did you give me fake promises?
Why did you give me false hopes?
Why did you reassure me?
Why baby?
Why did you let me get the plastic happiness?
Why did you just tell me you were not surviving?
Why did you leave me?
Why baby?
Why did you die?

Letter to Dad

MARGARET WAIRIMU WAWERU

It's been one year
Since you grew wings
But the memories are so vivid
The wounds a fresh cut
In my heart and soul

I understand
That you had to leave us
The pain was too much
And the angels felt like the pure
In heart should be in heaven

Mama still cries at night
I listen to her sobs
It really breaks my heart
But don't worry dad,
I will take care of her
Make sure she gets through it
And with time, papa,
She will be the radiant wife you once knew

Sitting in our dinning room
I witness your apparition on your favourite chair
You are smiling and waving at me
And for once I feel peace in my heart

We will keep the memories we shared and
All the cassettes we recorded
And when we feel sad
We will remind each other of where we came from
We will miss you for sure
But we know that
You will always be with us
Your wings will shield us from any impending storm

So, papa,
Continue resting in peace.

Missing Voices

UGOCHUKWU P. NWAFOR

(Inspired by Agboreko of Wole Soyinka's A Dance of the Forest*)*

Master and slave alike, of
Profound mischiefs, no ears
Still need be reminded that there
Are loftier messengers; restless
Rover of peaks and holes, my
Human ears are aware of its fate.
Yet if I ever venture into that
Forest which has been retold,
I shall invoke Agboreko for a walk.
Should I chance upon him?
Then you can tell that my eyes
Would glitter as though a
Goldmine's dream…But first
Things first, I shall bow my face
Towards the ground and mimic
His voice and that of history saying:
"PROVERBS TO BONES AND SILENCE"
Then I'd dare him to deny that though
The seeds of the last gathering are
Yet to break through the earth—loud
Enough to us as to the ants, as to
Make our dry mouths wet again
As in the days fast becoming nothing
But ashes of a previous night's
Fireplace—it must be known that
Some seeds are carefully sown
To never see the last light of the day.
But what stays dead forever Agboreko?
What escapes the eye that shall see all?

Now, centuries will no longer be

Needed for us to start living,
The feast of the living must
Become an everyday rite,
And we may circle all we
Want around his grim shoot,
But our hands will forever remain
Unfit to touch the Kingly Araba
Till we learn to carve more on the
Immense grace of our brutish minds.

Tears on Canvas

WESLEY MACHESO

How I wish we could paint
sadness on smiling faces.
Curve our lips into skulls
of loss
'til our mouths are canvases
of yawning graves.

There's no mouth to a grave;
it buries its wickedness in silence.
What voices scream beneath
those mounds of wasted minds?
Musings lost to the wind.
Bodies that become ashes.

But sadness is only painted
by life,
that wicked artist.

Nausea

WESLEY MACHESO

The dying embers of light
at sunsets
need not be dark.
Stars lie beneath the horizon
eager to illuminate the path for lost souls
knowing the giant has gone to sleep.
But who will guide the stars
through folds of raging clouds
when storms torment dreamers
waking up to nightmares of giants lost?
Who watches the watchers of darkness?

Oh, when I remember death,
that thief at dawn,
I puke what remains of my innocence.

This Easter

WESLEY MACHESO

For Easter we wanted to slaughter a goat.
Wash our tongues in the fountain
of blood sprouting from its torn flesh
in velvet rivulets of rose petals.
Men are born vultures.
But the world has bled enough
this year.
We have lost too much blood
and we are still bleeding.
No one else will hang
this Easter.

When I Am Gone

MARYAM ALI ALI

When you hear the
Death knell toll for me
Do not cry
For I do not belong
To this world, and
The world belongs
Not to me.

I will not miss the world
When I am gone
It has not accepted me
Nor I it
Weep thus for yourselves
That the world still has
You in its grip
I shall miss nothing
When I am gone

Nothing Has Changed

MARYAM ALI ALI

If I should die today
Nothing will change tomorrow
For nothing has changed
Since the last time my father
Breathed his last

It's the same sun
That rose the next day
It is the same moon
That sets at dawn
The same stars adorn
The skies

The same sun will set tomorrow
The same moon will rise with the tides
The same stars will adorn the firmaments
Nothing will change
If I should die today.

Protest

EJIOFOR UGWU

The morning came to me in voices
and footsteps: Sit down with your
little breakable life
and decide what you want to be.
And the sun was down.
But why does a morning like this wish
to make a poet of me?
I do want to be a poet
of sorrow. The world has wept enough.
I fed the voices with silence.
The plane crashed.
The plane also fought for its life
as we can see from the gullies
it dug through the mud while it fell.
The mud is there. Metal scraps
are there too.
The words at war in my head
are the same with the silent
speech of the mud and the metal scraps.
Why repeat a word well-said by the mud?
Yesterday, a man was shot in the head
in my country.
We say: what a pity.
The election has taken him.
And we move on.
But I picked up my pen to bring up
the words at war in my head.
They wear the scars
of the hurried moments.
They repeat the words
that have been said before.
And, oh, he is such a good poet, we might say.

And I would rejoice in your kind words.
I might even be crowned
for the words I have repeated.
I might be called to the gathering
of nobles. I might eat with the chiefs
at the dinner tables. I might marry
a good wife from my fame,
have good children. The words
still at war in my head.
The world still bleeding.
I want to write about flowers.
I want to write about the purple
blossoms of the bougainvillea.
And if they wither in the evening,
I will not cry because it is evening.
I want a good evening for all of us
and not the early mornings of our lives.

Our Voice is Gone

JANET JAMES IBUKUN

The Olubata has beaten the drum
But we say "Beat the drum"
We sight not the man of the moon.
The Olubata has beaten the drum,
We still await the man recounts history.
The Olubata has beaten the drum,
There is no dancer to dance us to reality.
The Olubata has beaten the drum,
There is no singer to sing the song of Justice.
The Olubata has beaten the drum,
Our talebearer is missing.
The Olubata has beaten the drum,
Who will pen our African experience?
The Olubata has beaten the drum,
The panting for our Aremo continues.
The Olubata has beaten the drum,
Our Pius has yet to pay heed to the call.

The moon is set ablaze,
The night is cold,
The day is bored,
Pius seems long dead.
I wish I became a spider Man
To save the plane of doom
Crashing our hero of truth.
I wish the wind could save the day
I wish life could be a rebirth.

In your grave literatus!
I see your beaming smile
I see the moving of your pen
I see those creative thoughts
Emerging in our reality!

You live on!
You live in your soulmate
You live in Damilare
You live In Tise.
You live in African literature
You live in every young writer
You live in me,
For I will pick the pen
Where you stopped.
Adieu to the star of night!

This time his smile beams in tears,
The sound of a flight draws his attention,
The tears in his eyes flow,
As he climbs the Ethiopian plane,
To a crashed dead land....
All we see in his loss
Is the beam of hope
That he lives!
His voice keeps lingering
"I did not die, I live."

Agadaga Iroko / Giant Iroko

SUNNY IYKE U. OKEIGWE

Agadaga Iroko rigoro n'elu ngwucha aka oru ya
Dara ada mberede nke ndu echefu echefu
Onye mana ikuku and elu ga-aburu ya ihe ila n'mgbanwe
Ha abuo kwere ya n'aka di ka ezigbo enyi si ekwe
Wee suharia dika egbe na ogankwu na-ebu n'ike

Wee buru ya lawa ala alotaghi alota
A na-ekwu na ozo mere, ozo etinye isi na-eme nke ya
O bu gini ka anyi ga-eme ozo-bu-iwe-anyi?
Agadaga iroko nkea alaala n'mberede n'atuwaghi anya
O mere anyi n'onu, wee gbaruo iyi n'obi anyi

O nwere aka gwara ihea dakwasara Agadaga Iroko nkea?
Ugboelu, o bu gini ka i na-adaghari?
Aka-mere-mere mere ugboelu nkea jee juo ajuju;
Ndi okwo na ndi nwe ugboelu nkea, ozoemela.
N'ihi na ndu di oke onu-ahia!

*

Giant Iroko

(Igbo: Translation)

The Giant Iroko who climbed the climax of his carrier
Had an accidental fall neither friend nor foe can forget
No one least envisaged the enmity of air and heights in this transition
Because they shook hands warmly like great friends with you
Only to fly swiftly, to sweep life away like kite and hawk

Conveying it far, far away into the land of no return
Enough should have known that enough was enough;
What shall we do to events that make the heart weep?
So, that's the end of you giant Iroko in this sudden departure!

Our mouths are amazed; our hearts are harrowed and heavy.

What deathlike hands conspired against this giant Iroko?
Why are you prone to kissing the ground airplanes?
Let your designers and builders ask you questions,
Let your pilots and firms command enough to be enough;
Because life is no cheap commodity!

This Poetry

JAMES TAR TSAAIOR

(accompanied with ritual drums)

This poetry. I write
Is a burden. To my being.

It weighs heavily. On my soul.
Like Elisha's. Yoked oxen.

A millstone. Around my ambitious.
Neck. A live coal. In my naked palm.

But I must. Write. Yes!
For this. I was born.

For this. I drew my first breath.
For this. I came. Isanlu's son.

Now I have. A blistered tongue.
Broken. And bleeding tongue.

Aso Rock. Applied a keen
Sword to it. I'm drained. Of words.

But my voice. Staggers on.
Down the whimpering. Valleys.

And up. The ascents. Of mountain summits.
With my head. Held high heavenwards.

This poetry. I write.
Is my covenant. With this land.

A covenant. Of abiding love.
A covenant. Of congealed blood.

I must forge. Unsung songs.
With the metal. Of my molten mind.

Songs that fire. The cold hearth.
Of the nation's heart.

This poetry. I write.
Is the just sentence. For this nation.

It'll stand. In final Judgement.
With this balding land. Of bragging bones.

That inhabit. The barren valley.
Of wilting. Dry dreams.

I must. Weave words.
Yes. Circumcised words.

To convince. And convict.
This brood. Of vile vipers.

Of their guilt. Running guilt.
Decomposing. Impressive guilt.

And cast. A hail of boisterous stones.
In the direction. Of gaunt Goliaths.

To mow down. The *Achans*[1].
In our ranks. In our desert struggles.

Who've broken. Our pitcher of oil.
And honey. And communal brew.

And declared. A season.
Of roguery. Of robbery.

Of our heirloom. Commonwealth.
To service. Their green greed.

This poetry. I write.
Will be. A boiling cauldron.

---

1. Tiv for a tree that usually inhabits the centre of the homestead, a metaphor for a household

In which this land. This homeland
And its princes. And princesses.

Will drown. In the stagnant.
Pool of their crimes. Guilt.

This nation. Is my cross.
My Golgotha. The way

To my Calvary. I must.
Walk the walk. Like a poet.

Possessed. By a prudent dream.
Foraging. For waiting oases.

To bury. A dimpled seed.
In a vast desert. Wilderness.

This poetry. I write.
Is my own. Golgotha.

But where's my sepulchre?
To rest. For three days.

To slouch. From the ashes.
Like the proverbial. Phoenix

And slough. To a new life
That is noble. And ennobling.

This poetry. I write.
Is my covenant. With this nation.

I will dip. The proud pen.
In wormwood.

Let it drip. Drip.
With bile. Potent bile.

This poetry. I write.
Will someday. Announce me.

To the world. Enclosed in another world.
To embrace. The smiling rainbow.

Beyond. The fleecy clouds.
Beyond. Towering silky cumulus clouds.

The Passing of Pius

UZOR MAXIM UZOATU

The passing of Pius
Unhinges the portal
Of my kernel. Manic,
I envision the curtain
By the edge of flight.

Nothing means zilch
In the forenoon of loss
As the meteor splits
Cracking up the cosmos
On the dot of finitude.

Up bounds protean wayfarer
Armed with a bent for lore
Hovering heavenward
Amid the hive of stars
Defining the divine.

In madness I make sense
Of the piercing passage
True to the testament of time
Upon a hallowed cremation
In the grave of my soul.

Light Dims to Shine Forever

AKACHI ADIMORA-EZEIGBO

I
An eclipse afflicted the arts house,
Fearful scourge not foretold by watchful seers
Peering attentively into the house of omen
Alas, its passing revealed that you had taken flight
To another world beyond our gaze.

II
You are light; you dimmed briefly to shine forever
You will always inhabit the literary edifice you erected
Your measured steps of success were phenomenal
Your gait echoed in the hallowed hall of honour
Eyes saw you, ears heard you and mouths uttered praises.

III
Many think you embarked too early on this journey
As if anyone knows when the journey would begin
Hoary, wise and witty literary ancestors welcome you
The youngest notable member of the griot clan,
You washed your hands clean. You dined with the greatest.

IV
Farewell, young but wise ancestor
Your glittering legacy will endure the ticking of time
Those left behind and future songbirds will remember you,
Wherever the torch of life is extinguished
There the stick must be relinquished –
Cold comfort this might seem,
But only the discerning can read the hieroglyphics of time

V

Mujee, mujee, mortals hastening to unknown destinations
Daring, challenging the inscrutable face of Fate.
Some may ask: what is the real import of life?
What is the use of all the striving, all the hours of toil?
Your life, your departure answered it all. Gbam! –
Man, woman, live well. Sow only good seeds for a good harvest,
Even if you don't harvest them, surely others will, after you

You Bled Africa!

MITTERAND OKORIE

"Mitt, my pikin!"
He would bellow, in that joyous,
Raucous laughter of his,
Which you heard from Nigeria,
If he laughed in Canada.
It was an African laughter,
Complete with its thunderclaps,
Its vuvuzelic rhythms

"Meet my pikin!"
You would tell them,
Leaving a young man to feel
That warmth, those jitters,
Which only
A Father's validation confers
This was a young man, you told them,
In whom you were pleased.

News of your death came to me,
Oh Prof!
In many shades of black gowns
It was dark on that Sunday morning,
Before it ever got bright
Transfixed in that cyclone of grief,
The wings of my heart flapped
In the stormiest storm it has ever seen

My heart still can't stand straight,
Many moons since you became one
With Africa's soil.
You thought, wrote,
And sang for this soil, this continent
My heart zigzags around,

In aimless flutters,
Nursing cold wounds of your demise,

I am stuck. Oh Prof!
In a never-ending circle of denial
So total, so effortlessly total,
That I suspect it may enrage you,
"Mitt, my pikin," I suspect you would say,
Get up, for the job of telling Africa's story
Must go on.
Must go on.

To the Muse of Isanlu: A Salute

'BIODUN J. OGUNDAYO

Adebola, scion of Adesanmi
Giant of Yagba, Yagba of Isanlu
You came, you inspired...
You proclaimed
Africa and Blackness
To be the center of our
Humanity
Resplendent in your fiery intellect
You restored, re-personalized our
Battered blackness
***
Regaling us with pungent mirth
Like the barbs of a practiced hunter
You celebrated Naija and Africa
Searing our sensibilities
Your sword of conscience and integrity
Re-centered
Africa
Naija
Us
Your people...
***
Your energies connected the local
With the global
Our apostle of boundless spirit
Undaunted, uncowed
You bestrode shores beyond
And havens within
***
Adebola, Omo Isanlu

Pius pious! Pious Pius!
In resounding clarion tones
You dared us to embrace
The virtuous, the beautiful
The eternal values of
Omoluwabi and Iwalewa
Yet...
You disdained facile piety
Embodying
Without turban, without toga,
Without soutane, without collar
Integrity so rare... so lacking
Even in priests of any faith

***

Your life celebrated
The best of us
May your death exorcise
The worst in us
That we may attain
The beauty, the integrity
The boundless possibilities
That you lived!

***

Happy trails, Adebola!
In galaxies
That excite our dreams...
Yonder
In the land of immortals
For you have earned
Your place
In our hearts and minds
Timelessly...
Eternally!

you remain with us

NKATEKO MASINGA

i wept at tinubu square
and the fountain water
seemed to gush in sync
with the fall of my tears.

Prof
we are yet to speak of you
in the past tense. to name
you in the universe of was
is a betrayal. you are here

in the books we read; your
children's memories house
your warmth, we remember
the anecdotes you shared.

Pius,
the reaper came to collect
and we ushered him in, not
wanting to deny hospitality
to any who came to our door

the reaper came to collect
and we ushered him in, not
asking who he was taking,
not thinking it could be us.

Pierced
we are by his bending sickle's
certainty, by the news of your
passing, an absence we feel
daily. an abscess in our core.

so we will never speak of you
in the past tense; naming you

in the universe of was belies
this fact: you remain with us.

A Bit of Narcissism

OKWUDILI NEBEOLISA

I had hoped this would be the last letter
I would write in the form of a poem
because I had begun to think that poems
written in the form of letters
had to be pretentious for their high language
which were required of every poem;
and then maybe a bit of narcissism

because of their confessional nature
which was required of many lyrics
but I realised that somehow these poems
had become like diaries of raw memories.
It was only here I could unclothe myself
and not feel naked, here I could be true
to myself and not be self-deprecating.

Bereavement

OKWUDILI NEBEOLISA

It was the end of mourning, my mother,
having returned from the funeral,
exhausted from the rituals she had been made

to perform to traditionally bid farewell
to her long-departed mother,
tried to recoup her financial losses.

Her face was illegible, a face
she only kept open to our sister
who had just finished nursery school.

There was no question our father would ask
that would appease her, no time it was asked
that was right, no tone that was used

that was correct, no words that were arranged
in the right order. It wore our father out.
Anyone would have thought that someone

who was mourning would turn to their lover
for the simplest of comforts. Before now,
we used to think that she was stronger

than our father, that if one of them had died,
our mother would be the one who would live
longer in the absence of the other.

One night I heard our father in the backyard
talking with one of my mother's sisters,
explaining the impenetrability

of the situation he had at hand.
It was as if he was about to cry.
My younger brother had been away

all this while in my sister's godmother's house,
preparing for his triennial exams,
so it was hard to believe whenever

we told him about this other's side
of our mother's personality.
It could be no more than a dubious story.

Imagining it was like finding a nerve
nestled in the thick forest of the skull.
She used to tell us how our grandmother

had been the only reason she visited
that idle place that was her hometown.
We didn't completely believe her

but ever since that funeral in March,
she has never found a reason to visit.

Dirge for the Departed

KOYE-LADELE MOFEHINTOLUWA

The mud of the house
Washed away with the heavy rains
The stew prepared in skill
Has finally become sour
The palm wine we kept in the corner
Liquor has spilled
Calabash turned on its face
The door of the house has fallen off
The night will be spent in terror
The home open to howls and cold
The house of the Chief Priest has caught fire
The divination board has burnt
How shall we speak to the gods?
The rain has fallen on the earth
But too much of it
Our houses are soaked in tears
Air Ethiopia flew away with it
The drum the whole city loved to listen to
Our drum has torn
Our smile is gone
Let us wait if another shall come
One who death shall eye but never touch
One who shall bring us fire

Prometheus that shall come from Olympus
Who will plant fire among men!

If Only

FEMI ABIDOGUN

If the harried hours
had waltzed slower
like a sluggish summer sunset;
the weather,
more clement
like a calm dove
and the wicked waves
billowed
a lot more mildly
with depths
like those of
receding ponds.
If the pliant "yes"
had been
a belligerent "nay"
or the eager steps
were staggered
and a tad delayed;
may be, just may be,
these streaming tears
drowning the face
would have been drops
of joy
rather than drips
of heartbreak
and dismay.

Falling Birds

YUSUFF ABDULBASIT

It's always a tragedy
When a bird embarks
On a downward trajectory

Like when the hawk
swoops to steal chicks
From a mother hen

Or when the pelican
Dives and scoops a mouthful
Of life from the sea

Or when vulture
Drops to feast on carcasses
After a bloodbath

Or when an airplane
Falls from high heavens
Like a bird catapulted

Broken wings
Nature has exerted her force again
"All that goes up must come down"

Good men are like fruits
They fall when they are at their ripest
Adieu!

Immortality

YUSUFF ABDULBASIT

People think immortality
Is trapped in vials

Vials that contain concoction
That can preserve our souls

Like formaldehyde

Some say cryosleep is the way
They dream that
Science will one day breathe warmth
Into their frozen hearts

A wise man said:
A good name lingers forever

Like the aftertaste of kola nut

That a good name is hoisted
On the shoulders of the tongue

Like a wrestling champion

One that has wrestled life
And defied the death of the body

That a good name is passed
From shoulder to shoulder

That as long as tongues wag
The name of The Pious lives eternally

Harvest of Deaths

YEMI ATANDA

A grieving moment lost
In the memory of reality
Of what exists, shall de-exist
On the rim of the Sun
Soft receding behind blank twilight, and
Peeping through from the darkling dawn;
Like in the cycles of births and deaths.

And the ravage of locust
Depleting the barn – this excrescence
Of worms in tubers – turns powdery
Of harvest of grains into air blown of waste!

The tall Iroko tree is the prime jigsaw
Of death, now the rafters
In the bellies of termites;
As prime in time the sawyer's
Tommy a home to worms;
As to replenish the eco-manure,
While the white ants aren't plaintive planks,
As the Caskets in the belly of the Craft!

Ah, look! Death is here, and lobes
Of kola-nuts, unsavory taste on palate
When the tendril is burnt in its tenderness;
And when the fountain ceases, everywhere dries up.

A few hours before the time, your ghost
Was lurking around the mind of Albert Camus,
As I read through the lines of your memory
In the acute dolor that lay in lavender!
Your paste in haste of my twirling eyes,
Hurriedly, Pius, you moved on like Abiku
And I called you just I did to Segun and Abolade,

Although they died unsung, unlike you, yet
Their graves have been turned homes to rodents.
Why is yours? I can only see flaring tongue of flames,
Igniting the world to lay wreaths upon the debris.
But all of you ignored my salient calls; willingly,
You crossed to the other side of the slender slivery stream!

Only you laughed at me: "Death touches all;
And the death of one, is one death too many –
Are you not now united in grief?"
Well, when fire dies, ashes cement courage
And when plantain dies, oozing sap
Reminds the living of truth
That at a time, each shall cross the bridge.

The Horse and the Tortoise

YEMI ATANDA

(With Talking Drum)

The race is here, and the race is here
Only the swift dare comes to the track

And the horse throttles in pride
In bridle of strength of princely ride,
Challenging all to a race, swelling rough
Like a monkey swinging on the bough.

The race is here, and the race is here
Only the swift dare comes to the track

Ruffle of air in the midst of all animals
As each looks at one, fizzling in trauma
When King Lion roars order! Calm and cool
Tortoise lazily craws to pick up baton of tool.

The race is here, and the race is here
Only the swift dare comes to the track

Ribs cracking laughter in delirious sputum,
But painfully delicate to kill a fly on scrotum
Like when bull locks horns with snail in a battle
It becomes measure of wits and courage in prattle.

The race is here, and the race is here
Only the swift dare comes to the track

Or don't think a mismatch on the ring,
A contest in weary spectators' ranting,
Matching feather weight with heavy weight
In digital race of global trade in height?

The race is here, and the race is here
Only the swift dare comes to the track

Now the race begins in fun-fare and fear,
The world lines up; misty air of dripping tears
As the horse girdles, and swift, while tortoise crawls;
Unknown a day, when wisdom is swifter than hoofs!

> *The race is here, and the race is here*
> *Only the swift dare comes to the track*
> *Which only time can change cosmic order!*

The Chorus Is Death

UBAKA OGBOGU

This is a song

The chorus is DEATH!

go ahead of your progeny
to a purgatory of your worst fears
offer cowries and precious stones
but remember — death does not eat wealth

DEATH!

ask for your memories in reverse
a chance to nurture the sprouts
a drink from rivers of tears
to nourish the void

DEATH!

misfortune preys on the fortunate
the fortunate pray for good fortune
and in the blink of an unfortunate eye
fortune yields misfortune

in the blink of a fast eye
bargain bin sorrow

AH!

DEATH!

where is his last stanza
where he says good night
where he serenades a nightingale

where he sees love and colours and blooms and history

where he wonders why a dazzling sun must set
because the gods cannot draw the curtains

DEEAATHH!

Breaking Bread

OBIWU

(For Igbeaku & Ihejianyaele, Mothers & Daughters)

Few are called, many are chosen
Blessed are the fruits of the fields
For they shall fill the land with warmth
      like the sun, moon
      thorns of brambles
      splashing springs
      and rolling oceans

Blessed are the rich in flesh and blood
For their branches grow, their flowers soar
They make songs and cries the lullabies
Of homes and playgrounds where we meet
Man and his neighbor, to break or burn bread
In the name of love or hate or all
We hold close to our bodies to keep us warm

Blessed are the many who answered
To a call that only a few actually heard
Who felt in their wombs truths that fell through walls
Suns rise and fall, dark drowns out the light
Toddlers throttle up and down toward the cemetery
The earth feeds and is neither lean nor fat
What the ears have heard, the eyes have seen.

Still They Hunt for Emmett Till

OBIWU

Still, they hunt for Till among the living.
After they kidnapped him from sleep
Stripped him naked, broke his body
Gouged his eyes, shot through his head
And dragged him down Tallahatchie River
In the cotton-gin fan they made him carry
Like a bedraggled mule in a putrid swamp

For a fistful of candy, wolf whistling
And the sole-witness of a fair maiden
Flirting behind a butcher's counter –
Sixty years after his murder sparked
A fire – they fret and froth over Money
And shoot holes into signs of his name.

on wisdom's wings

JUMOKE VERISSIMO

aluko bird said yours was not a departure
it said you rode the skies to a place
bodies become the conscience of men

aluko bird said yours was not a departure
it said you won't be back from this trip
where you rode on a cloud of ashes

yet, what do we call this trip;
        which is not a departure

there's a word that precedes departure
it is an assurance of a return
there's a word that precedes departure
it is the confidence that bade goodbyes
but what word precedes a man in the sky
flying on the wings of wisdom?

what word conveys a grief like yours
sitting on the ridge of our noses

ii
aluko bird said yours was not a departure
and we shouldn't accuse death of treachery
so, we won't honour death with our tears also.

yet, to whom do we tender a resignation
of how this voyage denies us a word to speak
we have no word for this grief
that insists it will sit on the ridge of our noses

we cannot speak of grief because you swallowed it
we cannot speak of grief because death honoured you
we cannot speak of grief because you left us words

nothing teaches us how to grieve
                    for a man in the sky
        flying on the wings of wisdom?

PART III
HOMECOMING

The Indent (For Pius)

UCHE NDUKA

1
Farther and farther out
from wall tiles. One shouldn't
belabour the bend with
oratory. With wavelip. With
a pick and a shovel. This
being at the mercy
of ambivalence. Of immanence.
Bluesing and moving to
a subdermal groove. For they
don't need restating:
silence, exile and cunnilingus.
Farther out: awaiting ecstasy
and lodestar. This avidity in
throwing cutlery at a lacquered
screen. Out of his nest feeling
neoned where vistas began.
Lineward. Lettered. Earthed. Guarded.

2
Because you asked
the sky for a dance.

Because you asked
for net and flint.

Because you entered
our memory

and sped up a trip
from head to heart.

Because you asked
where the barbed wire was.

3
The nation sits openmouthed
waiting to gobble up her own.

From a tangle of truckpushers
to jean-clad professors.

It's the same gourd anyway
the same mat
beneath a drumroll.

Getting back to the shrine.

I know we're asking
for a reunion, a homecoming

a crossroad in glory
the marriage of penguin and eagle
but it's no use

when the sun sets

ADEJUMO UTHMAN AJIBOLA

(To be sung and performed with traditional flute)

Kato r'erin, od'igbo
Kato r'efon, od'odan
Kato r'okin, odi gbere[1]

When the sun sets,
The poet doesn't go home
He rides on the wings of the wind

When the moon calls out night
To a tête-à-tête of loss
We listen to the rumblings of the wayfarer

The poet doesn't go home on shards of broken metal
No!
He stays around, hunkering
In ink and melody
On leaflets and music notes
On the ebbs of receding palm-wines

Wayfarer
Even when your footsteps recede
Your footprints paint the bedroom walls of our heart

Your flickering lights,
Like a candle, battling the scourge of the wind
Fans our embers of hope

Your laughter may not run amok

---

1. Yoruba: "Before we see the elephant, one will tread forests/ Before we see the buffalo, one will know the wild fields/ Before we see the peacock, eternity will fall upon us."

On the streets of our ears…anymore
But your words become our Bhagavad Gita

Pius,
You have become the aged *ose*
Death cannot kill
You are two hundred hills, rolled into one
Death scurries when the trumpet of your name is sounded

Wayfarer,
We are you
You are us
Death has refused us her home
We are Abiku
Killed, only to come back again
And again
And again
Even the shrapnel of a falling bird cannot defile us!

CHORUS:
Omo Adesanmi lo, mo lo di gbere
O darinako,
O digbere, o darinako,[2]

---

2. "The son of Adesanmi has gone, I say, till eternity/ Till we meet again/ Till eternity, till we meet again."

Aridunun Akowe

DAHUNSI AYOBAMI

That which cracked the land
Will bring out its head in no time
A child playing in the sand
And the rain says it is about time
A child that fails to take correction shall perish
An elder that refuses correction will perish

When the villagers formed a dancing band
Rejoicing with their false rulers
Like one hypnotized by a fairy's wand
Aridunun Akowe was there hither
To show them their folly, and whip their lords
He whipped them with his words

Though the villagers ignore him
His words still strike their hearts
We will change tomorrow
There is still a lot of time
Whatever we want to do time allows
Let us enjoy the life of our heads

Aridunnu Akowe answers: Foolish men
Time waits for no one
It is precious, take hold of it
Lest you die unaccomplished
Your weak ambitions are premised on false hopes
On and on, he whipped them with his words

Aridunun Akowe called a meeting of the elders
He revealed the secret of the elders
He made known the personality of Egungun
And the human devourers of sacrifices meant for Ebora
He brought a clear revelation
Of the society's soul

In agitation they shout
Aridunun Akowe is here, he is here again
Who are you to speak to us?
We are rulers, we are elders
Not giving it a moment's pause
Yet again, he whipped them with his words

All cried when they heard
Death has spread its wings
To take our dearly beloved
Throats were thick with phlegm
People, reeling in emotion, burst out in tears
Natives and foreigners alike

Death giving no one honor
Rich and poor, powerful and weak
We all must go
The great man suddenly flew away
Like the burst of an overblown balloon
His tragic demise remains a shock

Yet before, the dark horse he overcame
Nations still in distress over the loss
Cries over the game death played
The beloved humanist was pious
In our heart, still pious
Yet, he is gone

A man still lives
Even though he took the wing
And flew to the great beyond
His works live after him
Aridunnu Akowe still lives
Every day, we still see him.

Pius: Myth, Mystic, Mystery

TENIBEGI KAROUNWI

This is not a final curtain
It is the beginning of remembering
The birth of memories

Morning
Where the world has its foundations
The sun rises, filled with echoes of songs

The revered child knocks on the door of authority
Who dares?
Booms the prince of eternal youth

It is I who must embark on a journey
I seek favour, heed my request
Let my going be blessed

I bring my petition to the circle of playmates
I bring my petition in songs
Beaded gourds, clappers and sonorous voices
Let music herald my coming
And swinging waists cradle me in dance

SONG:
CALL: *Elegbe mo ni e je n pe lode eyi o*
-Playmates I beseech you, let me tarry on this outing

RESPONSE: *Iworiwo*

CALL: *Pipe at'eye lawo ti pepeye da*
-Long life and reverence were the duck's covenant

RESPONSE: *Iworiwo*

CALL: *Ogbo lawo t'orogbo yan o*
-*Longevity was the bitter kola's choice with destiny*

RESPONSE: *Iworiwo*

Call: *Ode akoko eni n wale iwara iwara*
-*On the first outing you hurried me back*

RESPONSE: *Iworiwo*

CALL: *Ode ekeji eni n pada iwara iwara*
-*On the second outing, you hastened my return*

RESPONSE: *Iworiwo*

CALL: *Ode eketa e je n duro n d'oota*
-*On this third, let me stay and become a stool*

RESPONSE: *Iworiwo*

In the realm of the unborn
At the borderline where hope dwells
Between the parallel lines of life and death

I plead my case with my ethereal mates
If I wish to stay, they must be placated
Playmates I beseech you, let me stay awhile

Mother waits on the other side
She longs for my coming one more time
Hope is forlorn, the world mocks
Tears cake her face

I must,
Yes, I must go again for a prolonged stay
My first entry was brief, you summoned
I heeded the call, I kept the covenant

My second entry was in haste
You said not to tarry, you summoned
I heeded the call, I kept the covenant

Each time, mother withers away
Her breasts shrivel, her glow dims
She's but a shadow, father is despondent

Playmates, I must go now, stay a while
Be appeased
On each visit, mother seeks to please

She makes rituals of love
Offers sacrifices in dance
Pays homage to those before
Even here, your table is laden with dripping fats

On the first journey, you hurried me back
On the second journey, you hastened my return
On this third, let me tarry and become a stool
Playmates be appeased, let me stay awhile
For a while, let joy nestle in mother's bosom

Though my time be brief
Like a roused meteor let it be fiery
A thousand years to come, let me illuminate still
Let my words spur action in timid minds
My exit, like explosive pods scattered in cosmic dust

The playmates came calling last July
But Oota was adamant, not in mangled metal
Not on a lonely asphalt, unsung in the dead of night

The playmates will be back
The book is opened

First, I must see the next birthday
Kiss mother one last time
Cuddle images I leave behind in a long embrace
Replica, words spoken, gifts shared
With these battle axes Ooootaaa finally defeats death.

Ferry man, wait a while
Let me do what I should
What I will, what I can

In this moment I have
In this time that binds me

I will keep the covenant
I return before the next cycle begins.

Returning the Light as Wreath

NDUBUISI MARTINS (ANIEMEKA)

I
Those feet that beat the paths
have taken the last dust—another breath to live again—not in same flesh, as sure as spirit spreading through all veins in seasons, places and persons.
I sing, lay the wreath
for,
Those ears, once erect at Isanlu, Ibadan, Louisville and Ottawa, the antenna of dia-tribes, coursing through many climes, now shrunken like harmattan leaves…
Those wayfarer's ditties, foraging the darkest noons, soon bring forth a new sun, disembowelled for light and darkness drained of fear.
Those songs retire to the night's pipes while silence makes a thud in Ottawa through Addis and Ibadan…

II
The one who goes is the chlorophyll of time and light.
Let life return to all shrunken bodies, for the one who goes as early dark seed, returns as long lightly shrubs.
On the season of dust, this daggering noon, this hanging tweet, wit-cache, drowsy memories this dryness bequeaths, let the rain spread green finger. The one who goes is the chlorophyll of time and lights to our earth.
I sing,
I lay wreath for the wayfarer of light.

Naija is a Badly-Behaved Poem

NDUBUISI MARTINS (ANIEMEKA)

Homeland, green for kleptocrats, is red in my verse —a poem written as an epic—becoming unfitting, over-sized sheets of noisy lullaby of a countryside.

The metaphors squeak rather than rhyme. Our poetry leaves many gnawing and a few looking through an awkward mast of meaning. Sound is a blast; quarrelsome vowels crunching consonants and vexed stanzas spit venoms...

A bad poem is:
A country of tribes 1914,
Lugardian convenience,
That fiefdom where
silence befriends oppression
and masses learn to live,
to adjust in circles of
ever-unfolding penury.
Naija is a poem, a badly-behaved poem.

Confessions of a Gypsy

RICHARD KAYODE O. JAMES

Because I know no other way to live,
I trust in gods

They take my soul in the air
And the flame of my body was kidnapped in the air.
In the air, I was thrusted into flames.

Because I know no other way to live,
I trust in gods

That my remnants burn the soil in which I was buried,
Till I am heard, by ears I punctured,
Before the air took me away.

Because I know no other way to live,
I trust in gods.

To heal your wounds, fill the heart of pilots with humanness,
That your children be clothed
And your road is fixed for human usage.

Because I know no other way to live,
I trust in gods.

I thrust you in the hand of activeness
That your mouth be troubled till you speak
And your pen trembles till the pilot evolves
And gift you with honorable flight.
These were my prayers then,
Before the air took me –

But because I know no other ways to live,
I trust you into my words and works.

When the Pious Die

UCHENNA-FRANKLIN EKWEREMADU

is it God holding a vacuum cleaner
above Planet Earth
sucking up the 'good seed'
for heaven's nursery
before he rains fire on the heap of chaff?

or is it nature discarding the pious
for striving to heavenise Planet Earth
and for striving to angelise the human race?

some swore they spotted
a fiery chariot on your rooftop
whisking you off to Abraham's bosom
there to be adorned with stars and stripes and
crowns and garlands
for the good fight you'd fought
in the never-ending war
(which has no room for fence-sitters)
between heaven and hell

Song of the Pilgrim

OBINNA CHUKWUDI IBEZIM

On this rocky, dusty, and rugged track,
trudging up the hill of life as a steeplejack;
though worn and weary, I face my travel
bedraggled and grimy, I still travail

On my brow is written the tales
of my life's struggles and rugged sails;
the turbulent seas of pain, loneliness and distress
inspire in me the hope of redress

Hunger and thirst have made me dizzy;
my vision has become hazy
yet I slog on, in this narrow path
of sorrow, ache and dearth

Overwhelmed by curiosity
men query me about my tenacity,
then say I to them: I have a blessed hope;
It is the gift that makes me cope

Despite my anguish and travail,
the light in my soul helps me prevail
from my heart issues songs of redemption;
songs that defy the tales of my dejection

It's only for a while; my journey shall be over;
mounting up on wings, on the skies I'll hover
at the sound of the trump, my form shall change
soaring up the heights, earth fading out of range

Pius, the Seed

CELINA O. AJU-AMEH

The Seed sown in hearts in the morning
Before jetting off 'on the wings of the morning'
These seeds moistened by the morning mist
When the afternoon comes offering the sunlight,
These seeds will sprout in the hearts and minds
And sprouting seedlings mature blown by the winds
And the heavens festooned with these stars nurture
The night bearing fruits from the pages matured
At the break of day Africa will eat the fruits from these
At the fullness of time the world will partake of these…
Aaa! "Except a grain of wheat falls to the ground
And dies it abides alone
When it dies it bringeth forth much fruits."
Aaa! "Except a grain of wheat falls to the ground
And dies it abides alone
When it dies it bringeth forth much fruits."

Cloud Coffin

TOLA IJALUSI

Water pot is broken, shattered
Into fragile fragments of fading future,
The mirror is obscure to the scenario
In performance of manly duty to self and pride.

Water pot is port to earth,
Lightning, thoroughfare to demise
Yielded to darkness, brim of loneliness.

You could have not gone yet,
Not yet, again I say not yet.

You could have waited to do what mothers do
See your daughters pregnant
Back your children and theirs
Sing lullaby and render wise words
Chant eulogy and bless us.

Vestige of mother's pot lies in soil
Vehicle by cloud coffin.

You've left for life destination
We're left to trail of love and patience
Built in discipline and confidence.

Letter to My Father

OLOLADE AKINLABI IGE

Father,
Yesternight,
I saw stars falling from the sky
and when they landed, they crashed.
Papa, do stars fall, too?

Father,
At the crash of the fallen stars
I saw drips of dew on the eyes of darkness;
At closer look, it was tears.
Papa, did the fallen stars take away breath?

Father,
At dawn, I saw the fallen stars all in ashes –
burnt beyond the visibility of the eyes
and every face around wore mask of sympathy.
Papa, was it a mournful morning?

I Journey Quietly Home

MARTIN IJIR

Today I hold my sun in my hands
without blaming why it stopped to shine
I end my tears as my air ends today
my soul watches the wreaths on the waves
like a spinning spider, love thread spun

inside me to embrace a new life
when dead takes my Sun away
it wipes the ignorance that held me captive
beyond the mud and shore of emptiness
I become refilled like a gas cylinder

a lasting air without blameworthy storm
I infuse inside me, praiseworthy sermons
this eternal abode, I traverse too without a fare
where psalms form a marvellous song
on my lips, my tongue becomes pure and divine

to recite unholy words unto the ears of God
as a blessed lotus I became on his threshold
elements pass by like scenic plains with palms
I am assured life in death as dying takes me home
unto a blessed way I journeyed quietly home

Hopeful People

NDABA SIBAN

in a future of hope
no one should enforce
upon a people a lifestyle
that lulls them into a state
of servitude and denigration

Explaining My Depression to You

YUSUF TASLEMAT TAIWO

On days like this
I'm the cause and I'm the cure
I'm the devil that dips his hands down your throat and brings out the words from your mouth
My anxiety has developed hands of its own and decided to crawl out from my mouth and engulf me in sadness
I committed suicide a thousand times jumping from my throat to the depth of my stomach
Yet, I'm still here.
God has a funny sense of humor
My panic attacks come in short and sharp stabs.
My heart bleeds for the love of my life who gets confused when I have my mood swings
I'm sorry but how can I tell him I'm just as messy as him
How do I explain that I'm getting too weak carrying his burden?
How do I explain that some nights I become a surgeon?
I cut myself into slices, small enough for him to eat
So, if he asks, 'what's for dinner', I'll say "Me"
Not in a romantic way but in a sad twisted way
Like a sacrifice being offered to the gods
I wrap myself with a ribbon and present myself to him
So, when he asks, 'what's for dinner', I serve him a three-course meal of me; Sadness, confusion and Broken. Do you like Your Dessert tonight dear?
Explaining My depression to my mum
She asks me "what is wrong?"
What is wrong is what is not wrong mum, let's say i have a "mild fever"
A mild fever masking the pain, rejection, the feeling of loss
How do I tell her that some days I feel like a band is having a

show in my head.
The noise becomes deafening and unbearable, but I can't make it go away
Explaining my Depression to my friends. First, that word doesn't exist in our lexicon.
All you'll find here is pure joy, happiness and whatever else makes you so happy that you wish you could bottle it and use it 3 times daily "as prescribed by the doctor".
So, whenever I feel myself slipping into the abyss of sadness
When my body gets too weak to go on
When the blade calls out to me
And the radio keeps playing my favorite song
Whenever my dead heart beats again and I feel like it's time for me to go home.
I take out my daily dose of happiness, open it and fill the room with its scent. I tell my demons not today.

Not Today.

The Broken Quill

NATHANAEL TANKO NOAH

                                                 Men
                                                        Are
    born
                                               Men
    die
                                    Here lies a great man
                                    Fallen
                       The mighty quill   is broken
                    The pot   is   dried up.
                        Suddenly
                The cat lies on his back now,
          Thrown down by the weak hands
         Of Fate.
        The mighty iroko is cut down
        By the hands of time.
     Here lies the chief of masquerades –
          Silent.
      This silence screams
    Unto distant lands.
   Tongues comment:
  The wind swooped
On
A
Lion
The mighty wind blew and set a sun.
Wind in the bamboo
  Hollow
  Stick
  On
The broken ogene.
   Mallet
On discordant xylophone

    The palm oil is missing
    How could these words be
    Eaten? In deed the handshake
      is gone beyond the elbow.

                    Kom, kom, kom
          Summon all the sons and daughters of the soil
                    Kom, kom, kom
          There's a gathering at the shrine on Konga hill
                    Kom, kom, kom
                 The gods are gathered
              Tonight a sage is deified.
               Our body hangs limp
                  Here we primp
                  the red earth
                        on
                    March
                  the tenth.

we do not know how to carry this pain

EDAKI TIMOTHY. O

at the place where the earth swallowed your coffin
i broke myself into fractions and crumbs and pieces
i sent a piece of my heart in with the coffin below
i sought for a place where hearts do not bleed
so i can place rainbows in my eyes and a nightingale's song in my lips
but pain is something we have not learnt to carry
this is why eons later we still find smithereens hidden deep in us whenever life tries to paint us the same picture.
you do not know how to carry this pain
my heart says sometimes
i try to stop my heart from beating sad songs and refrain my lips from carrying lonely lyrics in them
my shoulders dance painfully as I watch the coffin drop into the sands
but i am not the only one who mourns your absence
for we all haven't learnt how to carry pain.

Stars, Out

S. SU'EDDIE VERSHIMA AGEMA

The stars went out and so did the moon.
The singer stopped playing and went to bed...
– Langston Hughes, 'The Weary Blues'

The stars put out their lamps
Leaving the sky grey.
The moon, compensating, smiled meekly
A clear ball, different from yesterday's banana.
I stayed an eternity with you
But just as my heart counted a second
The night rolled away its mat
Bringing in the reality of day.

Converging Skies and Shadows

S. SU'EDDIE VERSHIMA AGEMA

We walked down a dried waterbed
our laughs echoed the emptiness of
steps printing us into the sands.

Suddenly, the skies converged
and you found your feet...
I found sounds that echoed silence.

The clouds covered the moon
as rains swallowed the grounds
and washed every print that was us.

II
I stand at the banks
Your memory is a spirit of the earlier silence
that keeps me company down dried waterbeds

III
I hear the voice of this darkness singing an invitation
I only see shadows
Stretching for a hug.

Shadows are my reality and I fear
This darkness has become too stark.

IV
Tiring, just before the final plunge
I wonder if all of us were passing seasons
gone
d
o

w
n

Will You?

BIODUN BAMGBOYE

And when all is stitched up in time
Processions marched, registers signed
When we all mourn and our tears run dry
What will be left? Who will you be?
Will you be the morning song of the early bird
The voice to waken the sleeping soul to a new dawn
Will you be the thuds of the *iya ilu*?[1]
Stirring our feet to the rhythm of the change he yearns for
Will you echo the voice of the lone hero we celebrate
A million echoes calling out a unified chant
Will you create a ripple in the river you flow
A million ripples creating a tidal wave of hope
Will your heart connect with poor and rich
Will you become blind to the differences of color and tribe
Will you dot your i's and cross your t's
Will you tread the paths
Of the humble Isanlu lad we remember
And bring on the excellence he lived for
Will you capture his smile and laughter
In the mirror of your soul and reflect it far and near
When all is said and done
Processions done, registers signed
When we are all mourned out and our tears run dry
What will be left? Who will you be?
What will you remember? What difference will he have made
To You, and You and You.

---

1. Iya ilu: the mother drum; the leading drum of the talking drum ensemble. It dictates and determines the pace and gives cues and prompts with its deep audible sound

Farewell

MARYAM GATAWA

the night has come
and my leave i take
bear me witness
the time has come
let the patient path
take me back home

before her moonless
threshold my path spreads
the shrubs are still
trees no longer sway
the world keeps quite
mourning my leave

the sea called me
and her path i took
tell the giant mountains
that my home is assured
tell the owls and her kin
now the night is hers

the fire is dead
embers do not glow
i am out of the ring
my gloves are off
i won't draw my sword
or fix my bow
i won't raise my voice
or turn back again

i must leave at once
before the sun returns
by tomorrow's dawn
my ship will be gone

what use is the hearth
when the fire is off
once the pearl is gone
what use is the shell
the sky looks bleak
cause the moon is gone

the night has come and
my pilgrimage begins
bear me witness
the time has come
let the patient path
take me back home

Transit to Kenya

ANTHONY ENYONE OHIEMI

Cold silence greets his walls
Stranded without the many daily slices
of his scarce hyper heroic intellectual tonic
Glaring at your debris battered and
Irked in thought by your mortal end
In the ultimate transit to Kenya of bliss
The world now booing Boeing
As casket of body bags
Drawn from the grave of the nosedive
Candles flame into the darkest night
Signed in the hearts of your mourners
In a less sane and deeply wounded world
Isanlu and Ottawa bowed in bewilderment
Of this departure that debits their dearest
As there is a void without a vapour
Tears without tame
Smoke without a smile
All for a
Victor of vanquish with
Crown from the crypt coasted to
Peace from the peril
Fly no more on the wings of Ethiopia
Only on eagle's wings with His
Right Hand leading you
Ad infinitum

Abiku Agba

USMAN OLADIPO AKANBI

Oota, why should I shed tears for you too,
when you refused to shed same for Maimuna Jimada?
Why shed tears for you too when I can bet that
the beauty of your works is ingrained on the marble surfaces
For all, and yet unborn generations to see and behold?
Abiku Agba, tell me why I should shed tears for you
when you too are cerebral generosity fixed in eternity?
Oh, pure Pius the pious writer, I have no tears to shed for you.
No tears because you are a legend your folks
can always proclaim to the world!
No Pius, I have no tears to shed for you too.
No tears because you taught us only one thing:
laughter in the face of adversity!
Ti oro ba ju ekun lo, erin la fi rin[1]

---

1. *Just a month before his demise Pius wrote a moving tribute to the late Maimuna Jimada. How was he to know that the poignant message he passed on in that tribute would equally serve him well at his own transition which was barely a month after. It is on this account that I decided to imitate the ending note of his tribute to Jimada to soothe his tragic exit from the terrestrial plains.*

Evening Bird

BAYOWA AYOMIDE MICHEAL

close to the sun, you embraced bluffs with serpentine fins.
You tripped the morose links of earth
    & tripped the heavens on howling wings.
// a poet; a feather//-
You became lines of sun-split stanzas & warped seas underneath you.
// a feather; a dreamer//-
You didn't have enough sleep,
& you ne'er dreamt.
You imitate a night-disciple;
woke, put out your hands and touched God in the face.
// a dreamer; a tossed coin//-
We saw in awe
as you burn blue through your gasps as balloons shudder
from the sight of a child's mother knitting needle.
& your gasps became re-run fireworks.
// a tossed coin; a fallen-pious angel//
Against the hard clicks of gong
& strikes of human-skinned drums,
the spotlight is moved to us; in thick tears,
& our tight gullets as a tourniquet.
We are displaced, cruising amid police gossamers
'**police lines, do not cross**'.
Our feet sweep feathers,
our hands with a kettle douche pools of grief;
one flops portraits & the other lanterns
on the debris that clasps our jean of locusts,
to melting plastics & iron shafts.

Evening bird,
as you watch tears rain from our eyes, please–
fall! fall!! fall alone!!!
like a thunderbolt faraway from our smiles

Withered Green

AUGUSTINE OGECHUKWU NWULIA

At first
The earth scientist
Newton, once spoke of
the earth's magnetic magic.

Then suddenly, we heard
Of green leaves falling off its nodes
Same way with frost petals
Dropping off the tulip.

Grandma once said
That only brownish-yellow leaves
Are chased away from the tree
'Cos they have become too weak to glow.

Are there still blossoms for pious mortals?
Cos if there is; then life is a pious gossip
Poised to mischievous antics and cruel treachery
That it took away a pricey Pius.

The other day
A shooting star furiously ran across the glowing sky
And sank itself into the thick clouds
Until it splashed darkness all over our faces.

Now, our eyes have become
Heavy again, and sagging
With angry fluids like
Sobbing babies with spilt milk.

A bird may fly wildly
On adventurous wanderings
But not with a fierce departure
Of no-return!

How do we replace a precious egg
That was broken, and
Shattered in daylight
Faraway Tulu Fara's 'Golgotha'…?

Quaking wonders have left us with
Swollen eyes and bitter memories
Yes! It's awful how a frost green leaf
Have fallen off the sky into the mouth of a dragon.

This whim; they call 'life'
Like a chameleon
That changes its colour
At the toss of excitement

Home Call...047

ONUCHI MARK ONORUOIZA

The orgy rhythm of the home call
Of an inimitable Trojan
With barely two score and seven seasons of sails and cruises
Upon the scorching earth
Left trails of an iconic footprint
The sudden call to roost
Of a lexical wingman, a scribal custodian
Whose scholarly tomes
Continue to ring louder at every passing day
It was a tragic tale of a lexical warhead who fought fiercely and fearlessly
The vile goons and gangs of credible governance
Now immortalized by his revolutionary deeds –
A radiant rose in a clime of thorns
Whose galvanic flight was truncated by darkened skies
Muffled by hazy clouds
And puckered by waffled wings
We would not forget how he groomed pullets and starlets of promise
His well wired path triggered evolutionary trends
Breaking norms, igniting embers of revolution –
He became for us a warrior of the wild
Evoking unalloyed truth to power
A radical crusader for the voiceless
With a purist passion for perfection
A ruthless apologist for the ardent activists of hope
His nuptial ardour with culture and humanity
Left for us an instructive reality –
To be humanely treated:
Humanise!

Outshining the Stars

ONUCHI MARK ONORUOIZA

Fertile realm scripted
Creative wit scribbled –
Sibilant notes gabbled:
With the most sombre rhyme
Of elegant lines etched with enduring rhythm
From the treasure trove of scribes conscripted
Of ballads like garnished salad
Beyond feeble visions and blurred dreams
Unlock eternal memories
Of Moonlight tales
Couched with boon songs of yore–
Reflective intersections
Of griots waddling folklores
With musings of radiant warmth
Like an endless stream
Glazed with tapestry of radiance
Conjuring plumes and garlands of conquest
An affirmation of the potency of words written
Words well woven outlast the vigour of the sun
Finely laced letters outshine the brightness of the stars
Lexical lines properly configured outlive the reigns of kings
Our words define us
Our words make us
As harbingers of witty tales waffle under the uptight sun
Words are made for us to forge with skill
Beyond the strength of steel
We master the craft of words with compelling appeal
An affirmation of our lettered zeal–
A signet of opulent seal
Farewell to a man of countless letters

The Eagle Has Fallen

MANASSEH GOWK

The eaglet is famished, her plumages are sallow
While the moon prolongs into dusk
Audience clad in crimson tattered cloaks
Drumming for a knight to return home
Who knows how far the eagle has gone
Who saw how great he plunged
I have longed to find his footprints
From the broken road that keeps us pining
Deeper into the woods and back
From the hills and valleys and thickets
Howling and wailing to hear his voice
But your death silently creeps into our hearts
Shadowy glances of your departure stings
As clouds gather upon your tome
Stealth as he comes to stir our fears
With garlands of your absence, it pacifies,
Spouting forth your heroics while you lived
Solace of your seraphic brevity beatifies forever
Fallen into our vivacious minds, your memory lives on!

Farewell

MANASSEH GOWK

A plinth stands alone
Bereft of a gargoyle
Forlorn of ever finding evergreen pastures
An African sun sleeps with its ancestors
Bygone with precious velvet flairs
An audience pays their homage
An endless ovation to the lost and beloved sage
Who sojourned with us on a Godspeed voyage
And reunite again at a celestial stage.

Death

KHALID IMAM

A cruel sword
Beheads the warmth
Of the fertile friendship
We share.

Now, wrapped in pain,
This agonizing truth
Leaves me
With the reality
Of missing your many
Laughter and hugs
Forever.

Sure,
No soul enjoys immortality
But the scent
Of your friendship
Is a memory
I shall live with eternally.

The Flood

KHALID IMAM

Call it a lachrymal poem
The drums from the grave
Are signs of grave dangers ahead!
Look up there: what do you see
Inside the sad eyes of the cloud, rage?
The wagging waves of the flood
Are enough warning to the wise.
Pray, do not trust the crocodile
Starved of drops of blood

Call it a lachrymal poem
The drums from the grave
Are signs of grave dangers ahead!
Say, I would not trust the pleasant sounds
The depth of a perfidious pond
Is not judged by its shallow banks
Alas, homes sink like broken canoes
Sharks feed on the heedless

Blue Skies

YEJIDE KILANKO

The skies were an ocean when we heard
words one wishes one can unhear.
Tectonic plates groaned
      as the world
           shifted.

We were stunned into silence
Reduced because we are less.

On these mean social streets, you earned your stripes
as you shared your light;
light infused into stories which conjured
what could be, what our people could be.

You told us greed sets the world on fire,
that stoic resignation stokes it.
We cannot be well when the futility
of fetching water with leaky baskets consumes us,

When the places we love continue to swallow us whole.
But we must love enough to question, to demand,
Like you loved
Omoluabi, o how you loved—

Final goodbyes are hard.
They sink fangs into soft places and leave gaping holes,
But something greater lies beyond the bright, blue skies
You. Have. Seen. It.

For years to come, we will tell your story this way.
One day, with majestic crown in hand,
You straddled a cloud and flew home.

This Very Goodbye

NSEABASI S. J. KING

That you were forty-seven and could've been seventy-four
Still there would've been no better time to say this goodbye
For like the good old wine you would've only become finer in taste
And we would never have had enough of you

That you were forty-seven and could've been seventy-four
Still there would've been no perfect time to say this goodbye
For like the graceful and grey-haired old thespian of great fame
We would've still had a role for you in the world is a stage

That you were forty-seven and could've been seventy-four
Still there would've been no right time to say this goodbye
For like the bright morning sun in its glorious shine yesterday
We would still be waiting for you with our new laundry today

That you were forty-seven and could've been seventy-four
Still there wouldn't be any other time to say this goodbye
For like the sweet honey that never loses its flavor even in its crystallized state
We make you this promise to preserve your fine thoughts in all that we do

The Deserted Road or Elegy for Pius Adesanmi

DANIEL OLAOLUWA WHYTE

> *He was buried without coffin*
> *Without a grave*
> *– Jared Angira*

when I hear the news that the whirlwind
ferried you to the land of no return
a sudden darkness engulfs the earth

the air grows pale
the time stands still
to absorb and sieve
this noise pollution, you cannot be dead!
not without bidding farewell to arms
like the gallant warrior you were
not evaporating silently in the still morning

but
your name has become a silhouette
your tongue – a sharp razor ready to shave
the heads of misguided rulers – is broken
your voice swallowed among discordant symphonies
is choked by grains of sand
alas! death has encircled your joints

the moon breaks into two
the stars ululate to the monody of your departure
the scars will not heal
your words will be a monument in our hearts:
"Naija no dey carry last."

What My Father Said on His Death Bed

GBENGA ADESINA

My father is beginning to die. Something inside him is slowly taking back every word it ever gave him.— Larry Levis

He said:
Sometimes I touch my skin
and I start to think I'm a river.
Then I start to think I'm a man.
What sort of man is a river?
But I'm a river. Or am I a man? I touch my face.
Why is the water moving?
Where is the river taking the man?

Wayfarer

JAMES YEKU

this final travel leads
to a home elsewhere, wearying innocence
with a flurry of thunderclaps
that scurry pain through tenderness;

through a heart harking
for father's return;
Words elude her;
Eliding fears
and the agony that tears

without end.

a flight of stars on the wings of mourning;
meteoric, the descent of an unwanted morning.

And there he is, flying away from us,
crashing into the void that riddles the living;

in and out of our thoughts; never
to be touched again,
nor heard once more, he of the roaring laughter.

And there he is, flying away from her;
with reluctance, his back turned
to those for whom his heart ached the most.

A lover's twilight.
A father's dusk,
heralding a cumulus of fears.

Ebbing.
Receding,
the voices that once assured.

And as rest to the weary,

The wayfarer goes the way
Of all flesh, to endless beginnings,

the primordial crossroads
of all branded pilgrims.

One Meets Two

JAMES YEKU

We rescue beauty from your ashes today;
dust from the dust that never was,
smiling out tears
to hide our fears.

We rescue beauty, and ourselves
from dreams and visions
of tiny footprints that color shadows
in the canvas of lonely hearts.

One
meets
two,
and they
both forsake three.

Mortals mounted by grief
for the pleasures of the eternal Other.

As we lay wreaths to absences,
we rescue you from the surreal gates
you almost entered,
knowing your dwelling belongs elsewhere,

where guardian angels, wild with warmth,
giggle welcomes to saintly souls
and whisper hope to us below.
That suffices us.

First Goodbye

D.M. ADERIBIGBE

The Principal came to our CRS Class,
unannounced as wind, to fetch four students.
He and his wife drove us in their new E-Class.
Be nice to him, as you will, your parents.

The principal said to us, as we shut
the door. The man was falling off an armchair
when we got in. Not surprising, since his hair
was a flake of morning sky and skin bought

by tens of wrinkles. He asked for our names
and blessed us. Told us what the years expected.
It's a price you pay. He asked for our names
and blessed us. Amen! We helped him to his bed.

Held our hands. His palms, scales of tilapias.
Bye bye my dear ones. He said and closed his eyes.

Monster

AFAM AKEH

Monster, monster, is that who you are?

Is that what you are? Are those
real horns and fangs and claws?

Do you beast people, make them howl
and growl, or feed them as grub

to their fellows? Do you crouch
in the dark and pounce on women?

What is this they broadcast
in loop in the all-day news?
   How is a beginning of promise so brutal
at end, all that salah gone to dust?

Will you not speak without riddle
this once to untangle my day?

Monster, monster, monster.

where you are now

RAPHAEL D'ABDON

where you are now
your name is still spoken
both halves of the trouble are solved
there is no hurry
no reversed question marks
no weakness for melancholy

where you are now
the eyes of science
open after the warmth of your myth
scurrying in-and-out amid the
roots-and-branches of art

where you are now
at the end of the labyrinth
with the oceans as companions
the patience of silence
gives to what you've made
rhythm and edge

where you are now
pulsing onward
creating figments
of suggestions and miracles
you breathe inside the words
you filled with absence and glee

where you are now
on the desert plains of midnight
there is a mirror on the wall
a willow down the road
a door beyond the ordinary

where you are now

to be a father is a nostalgic beauty
your children's faces
smile at you
from the midpoint
of baby flowers

where you are now
after walking the journey
you longed for
all you ask of us is to make
more than dust

When the Curtains Fall

UCHECHUKWU UMEZURIKE

She sits in the glare of dawn, curtains drawn;
   curtains, his fingers diurnally parted;

in the room the silences that clasp hearts,
the residue of his scent in the sofa;

the clouds a symmetry in the sky, their course slow
a fraction of how her thoughts loop in grief –

stripped of what is, what is the why, the what in what,
what is not, what is to be, what might be, what has become;

her face bears the fact of what was lost yesterday,
of what is joy & ordinary, what is beauty & brief,

of those to hold & lift up,
those to mourn;

there will be sunset, yes, & more sunsets,
shadows, too;
there will be snow & solitude,

lone music & broken flesh,
something nostalgic;

yet there will be tenderness
in what's left behind & the recall of love,

even after the curtains fall
heavy on our world.

PART IV
A SELECTION FROM PIUS ADESANMI'S *THE WAYFARER AND OTHER POEMS*

The Wayfarer

PIUS ADESANMI

(for Colby and Camille Nicholson)

What tales shall the wayfarer tell
When time and tide
And the pull of ancestral blood
Return him to his native land?

Shall he tell tales of igloos
Of temperatures congealing his tropical blood
Of bills and more bills:
Hydro, cable, MSP, phone?

When accomplished and fulfilled
I bid farewell to the ice of Canada
To fry anew
Under African skies

I shall tell tales of love
Found in the jungle of the Nicholsons

I shall tell tales of nuptial fires
Stoked by Colby's bacchic rivers
Of Phil's irrepressible jokes
Of Rosie's furry caresses
Of Iain's computer romps
Of blossoming petals: Shonet, Sheron, Sheila

Colby's "white sons of a bitch" and "black bastards"
In a communion unburdened by history

Camille's smiles fresh and foamy
Like Bàbá Ẹlému's undiluted morning harvest

Yes, I shall tell tales

Of Stanley hosting Mutesa
In the absence of blood and cannons

(Quesnel, May 2000)

Ah, Prometheus!

PIUS ADESANMI

(For the victims of the oil pipe explosion in Jesse, Nigeria)

Ah, Prometheus! Cursed be the one Zeus appointed
Watchman over your rocky gulag in the Caucasus

Did he partake of the gods' bacchanalia
Drifting to sleep in some Maenad's bosom
While you yanked off your chains, authored another heist?

Did the vulture have his fill of your liver
Leaving you to uncatholic designs?

Now I hear you've drifted far away
Fugitive, snaking your way and your loot
Through Shell's medieval pipelines
In my homeland

        gbosaaaaaaaa!!!

And the farm lands became Hiroshima
The fishing Deltas challenged Nagasaki
Women, children, a thousand civilians roasted
Vultures don't always like their meat raw
A fetal tenderloin steak is a great treat

        and there is no more Ken to pen the dent

Wily son of Iapetus
Return then to Olympus
Render unto the gods your loot
And let my people feast in peace
At the next oil leak festival.

Odia Ofeimun: The Brooms Take Flight

PIUS ADESANMI

Because in his land

- politicians disembowel the central bank
- generals milk Deltas for foreign Molochs
- professors profess ossified theories
- students spit on textbooks, kiss the bottle, AK47 in hand
- ṣàngó's recipe for light remains a mystery
- public taps belch continuously in their emptiness
- newly weds, deaf to ministerial sirens, become macadamised pulp
- òjgún forges ferrous pythons in front of petrol stations
- ayatollahs decree drunken orgies of limb-chopping and public flagellation
- 120 million corpses pretend to live

Because in his land:

- he tried to dream and was told
  that the generals were allergic to dreams

Because in his land:
- a poet lied

Because his is a land of unending becauses
He dusted his gong, like the town crier in my village

Ko! Ko! Ko! Ẹ Wokun O! Ẹ Wokun O!
(We need new brooms
to clear the rot
and renew our lot)

Because in his land –

    Those who have ears are:
    – too hungry to hear
    – too angry to care

He went to work
Crisscrossing deltas and savannahs
In search of tender palm fronds
Which he found in abundance
In Ibadan, Lagos, Nsukka

He dried and threshed the palm fronds
And made new brooms
He examined his work
And saw that it was good

But his brooms, unable to sweep
Because...because...because...
Attached themselves to a stick
And the broomsticks took flight

Here we are his new brooms
Warming frozen verses in wintry winds
Sweeping already swept Ivory Towers
In Germany, Britain, America, Canada

(Those at home await their turn to fly)
I phoned the maker of brooms yesterday
Yanked him from the auroral grip
Of his imagination at work
"Ah, you foolish boy! When are you coming home?
We have work to do."

The zombies are back in their lair
And his dreams are back at work
May they not encounter *Ọláreyín*
On their path to fruition.

To the Unfathomable One

PIUS ADESANMI

(After a telephone conversation with Nduka Otiono)

Soul brother of horrendous desires
Blood brother, decked in bohemian attires
Here I come again
The one whose name you feared to call
Groping for the door-knob
To the sinewy cave of your mind
Where Daedalus hones his craft

I have opened up
And for you who is part of me
I consecrate this song
JUST THIS ONCE

I should have taken you seriously
When seized by a Gulder-aided nocturnal inspiration
You hatched those lines in Crowther lane
Georges and Otiono snoring on slumber lane

I am part of you but blinded by your mystique
And as I confront your secret
Passage to India in these frozen climes
Fermat's last theorem becomes child's play

Open up that soul brother
Crack the kernel of secrets grown fetid

Part ways with your friend the ostrich
Listen more to the brother from Íkéré Ékítí
For man can only mean to man
Brother to brother
In the absence of darkness

Message from Aso Rock to a Poet in Exile

PIUS ADESANMI

1

Your grandfather is a pain in the ass
Self-appointed flusher of imaginary morass

He held up a radio station
Screaming of a doomed nation

He raved he saw an open sore
And disturbed our giant snore

We asked him to fend death off our roads
He roamed Western capitals, croaking like a toad

2

Your father, ah, dat one was worse
Small pikin, shouldering a foolish cause

He abused his elders, calling them vultures
A so-called man of culture

He shelled Shell's dollar-spinning pipes
His lips married to his own pipe

We invited him to come and eat
He clung to a pen, clung to shit

3

You, having ventured under Northern skies
Please, remain there in your cage of ice

Ọjá Óyíngbó, beseeched by a million haggling voices
Never notices the absence of one tardy trader

Entries

PIUS ADESANMI

I headcrashed into this world
Tearing through the thighs of a wailing woman
I headcrashed into this world
Biding my amniotic bliss: see ya!

Olayinka Adesanmi. So they branded me
Eight days after my first coming
Saw me alight in Isanlu
Pyrrhic relief to her whole womb
Authored two previous female passages

One peep into their anarchy
One peep in their wars
I dialogued with my limbs
And retraversed the realm of the Beyond

Asaro was at the threshold
To welcome me back
Leading a theory of cynical goers and comers
Pitiless harvesters of maternal tears
I brought them glad tidings
Of another household anguished

Four harvests later
I ventured a second entry
Via the same hopeful womb. Music from
Her rosary beads dulled my reflexes

They rejoiced. Behold another preserver of the lineage
Entering with fanfare, drying the river of tears
This time they named me for the pope
As I took note of exit routes

Alas! Bàbá Alábẹ's blade was swift
The number eleven chiselled on each cheek

Chained me to this realm of wars
No blemished skin can find
The secret door to Asaro's Higherworld

Earthlings, among you I'm a prisoner of war
Escape. Escape is always on my mind.

PART V
POSTLUDE

A Prose-Poem, a Tribute, and a Wreath for Pius Adesanmi

ANU'A-GHEYLE SOLOMON AZOH-MBI

On behalf of the Group of African Ambassadors[1], High Commissioners and Chargés d'Affaires in Canada, I thank the authorities of Carleton University for the honour to be here today.

The Algonquin peoples on whose traditional territories we stand today share so much in common with our African ancestral peoples – Both are a drumming and dancing people.

At the birth of new life, we dance;

At the passing of an old person, we dance;

At the coming of the rains that soften the fields for planting, we dance;

When happy with the harvest or the hunt, we dance;

When the soul is moved with pity for the widow and orphan next door, we dance to bring comfort and cheer…

Every day and every occasion is a festival of life – life in which death is only a part, in fact death is seen to be a mere continuation of life in a different form and in a different realm.

---

1. A Tribute delivered at the Festival of Life in honour of Pius Adesanmi at Carleton Dominion Chalmers Centre on March 26, 2019. Anu'a-Gheyle Solomon Azoh-Mbi is Cameroon's High Commissioner to Canada and Dean of the Diplomatic Corps in Canada.

Thus, in our celebration of life, we celebrate alike the gifts of joy and of sorrow.

We drum and dance not only to celebrate the ultimate gift of life; but to celebrate the Creator, the giver of all greater and lesser gifts. It is an acknowledgement of the Creator's sovereign sway over the seasons and over the affairs of mortal man,

Therefore, let this festival of life in honour of the late Professor Pius Adesanmi, be for us an occasion to show gratitude for the gift of life and for the grace to live out that life.

Let this celebration be for us an exercise in the ultimate education of the soul. Let it awaken us to the timeless values and virtues of truth and wisdom, honesty and humility, love, respect and courage without which our lives are poor and worthless.

As Director of Carleton University's Institute of African Studies, Professor Pius Adesanmi sought to build strong synergies with members of the African diplomatic Group in Canada toward improving Canada-Africa relations.

Professor Pius Adesanmi was a man of spirit, full of courage and animated by the general good. He was a happy humorous soul. He was energetic, eloquent, engaging, and driven by excellence. His was a free, frank and fearless spirit. He was a lover of truth and wisdom. He was honest in his assessment of the human condition. He was humble and kept the common touch. We were delighted to know and to work with him and are all saddened by his untimely demise.

Prof. Pius Adesanmi left us too soon at barely 47 years of age, but his voice and values, his words and works will continue to vehicle to future generations the vision of a bold new world in the making. He did his part. Let us each endeavor to play our own part as we rise from here.

"A long life may not be good enough, but a good life is long enough," says Benjamin Franklin.

Last week, someone sent me a post on social media that read: "The most wonderful places to be in the world are in someone's thoughts, in someone's prayers, in someone's heart."

What a better place for us to keep Professor Pius Adesanmi! May his family and friends find comfort in knowing that the best memorials to this extraordinary soul are inscribed eternally in the hearts of all who knew and loved him.

When and If...

PAMELA J. OLÚBÙNMI SMITH

When the river of our tears begins to ebb,
And we slowly begin to see our way clear…
When we hear the wind blow,
And we swear we just caught a glimpse of you dancing in the wind.
When it finally dawns on us that you are not returning from the journey you took,
And we finally realize that the "goodbye" at the door this morning is indeed the last one.
When the last of the mourning guest bids us adieu
And we close the door gently behind us.
When in the deafening silence
We realize there shall be no more dance.
Dear Pius, it is time to whisper in God's ear:
"Lord, cast thy countenance on all whom I love and left behind."
AMEN!

Contributors

Abasi, Iquo Diana is the author of *Symphony of Becoming*, which was shortlisted for The Nigeria Prize for Literature and the ANA poetry prize respectively, in 2013. This collection was also shortlisted for the Wole Soyinka Literature Prize in 2018. Daina Abasi has performed in the Lagos International Poetry Festival, Ake Arts, Wole Soyinka @80, Lagos Black Heritage Festival, and PLAY Poetry Festival.

Abdulaziz, Abdulaziz started out as a creative writer and newspaper contributor before he picked his first journalism job in 2007. He has worked in different roles within the media, both in Kano and Abuja. Abdulaziz is associate editor at the online newspaper, *Premium Times*. He was awarded the Wole Soyinka Prize for Investigative Reporting in 2018.

Abidogun, Femi is the author of two poetry collections, *That Long Walk* and *Blonde Grass*. He has performed his poetry at the Birmingham Literature Festival, Shrewsbury Festival of Literature, and Celebrating Sanctuary Festival as well on the BBC West Midlands radio. Abidogun lives in England.

Aderibigbe, D.M. is a Nigerian doctoral student at Florida State University, Tallahassee, United States. His first book *How the End First Showed*, won the 2018 Brittingham Prize in Poetry, and a 2018 Florida Book Award. He has received fellowships from the James Merrill House, OMI International Arts Centre/Ledig House, and a Robert Pinksy Global Fellowship.

Adesanmi, Pius was a Nigerian-born Canadian writer, scholar, professor of Postcolonial African literature and Director of the Institute of African Studies at Carleton University, Ottawa, Canada. His first book, *The Wayfarer and Other Poems*, won the Association of Nigerian Authors' Poetry Prize in 2001. His collection of essays, *You're not a Country, Africa,* won the inaugural Penguin Prize for African Writing in the nonfiction category in 2011. His collection of non-fiction writings, *Naija no Dey Carry Last: Thoughts on a Nation in Progress*, was named The Channels Television Book of the Year. In 2017, Adesanmi received a Canada Bureau of International Education

Leadership Award. He was one of the victims of the crashed Ethiopian Airlines flight 302 of March 10, 2019.

Adeshina, Adesanya Adewale is studying for a Bachelor's degree in English Language at the University of Lagos, Nigeria.

Adesina, Gbenga jointly won the 2016 Brunel International Poetry Prize for African Poetry. He has received fellowships and scholarships from Callaloo at Oxford, Poet's House New York, the Norman Mailer Center, Fine Arts Works Center, among others. His works have appeared in the *New York Times, Washington Square Review, Prairie Schooner*, etc. Adesina is a GoldWater Poetry Fellow at New York University.

Adimora-Ezeigbo, Akachi has taught at universities in South Africa and the United Kingdom and has delivered lectures in the United States. She has been awarded Visiting Fellowships in the United Kingdom, South Africa, and Germany. After many years of teaching at the University of Lagos, she is now a Professor at Alex Ekwueme Federal University Ndufu-Alike, Ikwo (AE-FUNAI), Nigeria. A prolific writer, she has published in various genres of literature as well as in academic writing. Adimora-Ezeigbo is a Fellow of Nigerian Academy of Letters.

Agbo, Joshua obtained his Ph.D. in African literature from Anglia Ruskin University, Cambridge, United Kingdom. After his post-graduate programme, he taught Undergraduate, MPhil, and Ph.D. students at the University of Cambridge, before returning to Nigeria to teach at the Benue State University, Makurdi, Nigeria. Agbo is the author of *How Africans Underdeveloped Africa: A Forgotten Truth in History, Dead Wood*, as well as the co-editor of *Linguistics: An Introductory Text*.

Agema, Agatha (née Aduro) holds an MBCh.B from Obafemi Awolowo University, Ile-Ife, Nigeria, and a Master of Science in International Health from the University of Leeds. Her prose pieces have appeared in various publications such as *A Basket of Tales: a Benue ANA Anthology of Short Stories* and *Saraba Magazine*. Agema is the author of *The Enchanting and Other Poems*, a chapbook available for free download online, and was one of the pioneer content providers for *Wawa Book Review*.

Agema, Su'eddie Vershima is President of African Writers at the University of Sussex. He is the author of four poetry collections including, *Home Equals Holes: Tale of an Exile* (Winner, Association of Nigerian Authors Poetry Prize 2014 and Nominated for the Wole Soyinka Prize for Literature 2018), a children's book, *Once Upon a Village Tale* and a short story collection, *The Bottom of another Tale*. Agema also won the 2016 Mandela Day Short Story Prize.

Agozino, Biko is the author of several books including *Critical, Creative and Centered Scholar-Activism*; *Today Na Today* (poetry); *The Debt Penalty* (playscript); *Pan African Issues in Crime and Justice* (co-edited), and *Counter-Colonial Criminology*. Agozino was the Director-Producer of *CLR James: The Black Jacobins Sociology Series*, and Director-Producer, *Shouters and the Control Freak Empire*, which won the Best International Short Documentary, Columbia Gorge Film Festival, USA in 2011.

Agyakwah, Fareed also known as Kente Agyakwa, is an essayist and columnist. Agyakwah's work has been published in *The Harmony: Indo African Footprints*, *Setu Journal of Arts Literature and Culture*, *Indology*, and elsewhere.

Agyeman-Duah, Ivor is Director of the Wole Soyinka Foundation at the University of Johannesburg, and chair of the Advisory Board of the Heritage and Cultural Society of Africa. A literary historian, he is co-editor of *Crucible of the Ages: Essays in Honour of Wole Soyinka at 80* and was Co-Director of the 55th Memorial Anniversary of the Makerere Conference of African Literature with the School of Oriental and African Studies, London, University of Johannesburg, Goethe Institute in Accra and the British Council in Kigali. He is also editor of *All the Good Things around Us* and *The Gods Who Send Us Gifts*.

Aina, Tade, formerly a professor of Sociology at the University of Lagos, is the Executive Director of the Partnership for African Social Governance and Research based in Nairobi. He has served as Program Director, Higher Education in Africa, at the Carnegie Corporation of New York, and Regional Representative for East Africa at the Ford Foundation's Nairobi office. He has also served as Deputy Executive Secretary of CODESRIA. Aina serves on the Kenya Human Rights Commission and the board of Winrock International.

Ajala, Adesina trained in Medicine and Surgery from Ladoke Akintola University of Technology, Ogbomoso, Nigeria. His short story was a joint winner of The Shade of Women Foundation Writers Prize for 2018. Ajala lives in Gusau, Zamfara State, Nigeria.

Ajeluorou, Anote heads the Politics desk of *The Guardian*, Lagos. Prior to his current appointment, he was Assistant Arts Editor of the newspaper. He is the author of a story book for children, *Igho Goes to Farm*. Ajeluorou also coordinated an anthology of short stories, *Moonbeam*.

Ajibola, Adejumo Uthman is a Master's student at the University of Ibadan and also an editor, playwright and screenwriter. He is the 2014-second runner-up of the Christopher Okigbo Poetry Prize organized by the Poetry Club of the University. He has served as the President of the Christopher Okigbo Poetry Club, University of Ibadan. His work has appeared in *ANA Review*.

Ajima, Maria is a senior lecturer in the Department of English, Benue State University, Makurdi, Nigeria. She won the Association of Nigerian Authors (ANA)/Spectrum prize for prose with her manuscript titled *The Survivors* in 1996. Ajima was also an African Regional runner-up in the 2000 commonwealth short story competition with her short story titled *Mother Mine*.

Aju-Ameh, Celina O. holds a Bachelor of Science/Education in Biology Education and a Master of Science in Applied Entomology and Parasitology from the University of Jos. She is in her final year of a PhD in Entomology and Parasitology. She has published several science research papers in international journals and a book on *Aedes aegypti* mosquitoes. An Oxford-trained counsellor, Aju-Ameh is a Director with the Shelter for Abused Women and Children (NGO) and also an Intercessor with Huldah's House Support Initiative.

Akanbi, Usman Oladipo is a lecturer in the Department of Agricultural Economics and Farm Management, University of Ilorin, Kwara State, Nigeria.

Akeh, Afam is the author of *Letter Home and Biafran Nights* and *Stolen Moments*. He has performed, broadcast and workshopped his poetry at literature events, the BBC and various UK school-related events and programmes, including a workshop event for the Oxford University Poetry Society. Akeh's *Letter Home and Biafran Nights* was longlisted for the 2013 The Nigeria Prize for Literature. He lives in Oxford, U.K.

Akinlabi, Peter's collection of poems, *Iconography,* was shortlisted for The Nigeria Prize for Literature in 2017. He earned a Bachelor of Arts from the University of Ibadan and a PhD from University of Ilorin, Nigeria. He is the author of *A Pagan Place*, published under African

Poetry Book Fund chapbook box set series: *Eight New-Generation African Poets 2015* published by Akashic Books. Akinlabi lives in Ilorin, Nigeria.

Ali Ali, Maryam is a lecturer in the Department of Islamic Studies, Saadatu Rimi College of Education, Kumbotso, Kano. Ali is a bilingual novelist (Hausa and English), publisher and poet.

Aliu, Kennedy Hussein is a Nigerian-Canadian poet and student in Ottawa, Canada. In high school, Kennedy received an award for Best Spoken word poet. He is a strong believer in telling stories through poetry and has extreme curiosity for oral histories, and historical preservation.

Aluko, Funmi is a poet and playwright. She is the author of *Rhythms From My Dimpled Backside (poems)*. She has worked as a journalist and volunteered with youths and vulnerable children in correctional homes for over two decades through her organization, Pathway Initiatives. She is a fellow of Ebedi International Writers Residency Nigeria and of OSIWA Poets Residency, Goree Island, Dakar, Senegal. Aluko serves as the Treasurer, PEN International, Nigeria Center.

Arellano, Leyda Jocelyn Estrada graduated from Carleton University with a Bachelor of Arts in English Literature in 2019. She is a poet and community collaborator originally from Mexico, raised in Texas, and living in Ontario. Arellano is an ardent believer in empowerment for vulnerable people and volunteers in community-uplifting causes and activities.

Atanda, Yemi is a playwright, director, poet and essayist. He holds a Master's degree in dramatic theory and criticism from the University of Ibadan and a PhD from the University of Ilorin.

Ayobami, Dahunsi is a graduate of English (Education) from the University of Nigeria, Nsukka (Ikere Ekiti Campus). She is working on her first anthology to be published in 2020. Her passion includes a deep love for languages and creative arts. Ayobami lives in Ibadan, Nigeria.

Azino, Efe Paul is a performance poet. He is founder of the Lagos International Poetry Festival, and director of Poetry at the annual Lagos Book and Art Festival. A fellow of Osiwa Poetry Residency, he is the author of *For Broken Men Who Cross Often* and *The Tragedy of Falling with Laughter Stuck in Your Throat*. He is also the producer of the spoken word poetry theater production, *Finding Home*.

Azoh-Mbi, Anu'a-Gheyle Solomon is Cameroon's High Commissioner to Canada and Dean of the Diplomatic Corps in Canada.

Azuah, Unoma is professor of English at the Illinois Institute of Art, Chicago. She recently published *Blessed Body: Secret Lives of the Nigerian LGBT*. She has won the Aidoo-Synder Book Award, Spectrum Book award, and the Hellman/Hammet award.

Azuonye, Nnorom is the Founding Publishing Director and Chief Executive Officer, SPM Publications, London. Editor of *Sentinel Literary Quarterly*. He is the author of *Funeral of the Minstrel*, *The Bridge Selection: Poems for the Road*, and *Letter to God & Other Poems*. Azuonye's essays, short fiction, poems, and interviews have appeared in *Agenda, Orbis, Eclectica, Flair, World Haiku Review* and *Maple Tree Literary Supplement*.

Badeji, Susan Bukky is a lecturer in the Department of Theatre Arts at Redeemer's University, Ede, Osun State, Nigeria. She holds an M.A. degree in Theatre Arts from the University of Ibadan, and specializes in African Theatre and Design (Costume and Makeup). Badeji enjoys public speaking and lives in Ibadan, Nigeria.

Bamgboye, Biodun is a development consultant and entrepreneur. She holds a B.Sc. in International Relations from the University of Ife and has acquired professional certification from international institutions including the University of Birmingham. Bamgboye has volunteered with United Nations Online Volunteers, and lives in Belgium with her children.

Bayowa, Ayomide Micheal transferred from the University of Ibadan to University of Toronto, Canada, to complete his undergraduate studies. Bayowa is the author of *Stream of Tongues*, *The Watercourse of Voices,* and *How to Break Loose from the Battlefield* which was longlisted for the 2018 Nigerian Students' Poetry Prize. His other poems such as "Terpsichore" was shortlisted in the 2019 Christopher Okigbo Inter-university Poetry Prize while 'If Only' was shortlisted in the 2019 Eriata Oribhabor Poetry Prize. Bayowa is also an actor and cinematographer, and lives in Toronto, Canada

Bello, Abiodun is a teacher and researcher. He is winner of the Okigbo Poetry Prize at the University of Ibadan in 2005 and a recipient of the Departmental Prize of the department of English at the 59th convocation ceremony of the University of Ibadan. While his research has been published in various journals, Bello has served as

Production Editor of *Ihafa: A Journal of African Studies* at the University of Lagos.

Bolton-Akpan, Tijah finds time to write when he is not busy working with communities and government to promote citizen-centred development. He lives in Calabar, Nigeria.

Bryce, Jane is Professor Emerita of African Literature and Cinema at the University of the West Indies, Cave Hill (Barbados). She has published cultural and literary criticism in a range of academic journals and essay collections. Formerly a freelance journalist and fiction editor, Bryce is also a creative writer and has recently completed a memoir of Tanzania.

Chami, Nidhal is a lecturer at the Faculty of Foreign Languages, University of Oran 2, Algeria. She teaches African literatures and is a member of the laboratory: Laboratoire de langues, littérature et civilisation / Histoire en Afrique. She is working on a project on the role of Algerian women fighters during the Liberation War and plans to write a collection of stories recording the Moudjahidate's testimonies. Chami is the author of the poetry book "é CRI t s du Coeur".

Cole, Soji is winner of the 2018 The Nigeria Prize for Literature and the Association of Nigerian Authors' Playwriting Prize, 2014. He has been a Fulbright Scholar at the School of Music, Theatre and Dance of Kansas State University, Manhattan, Kansas, USA, and a Creative Writing Visiting Fellow at the University of Roehampton. Cole is an instructor of Playwriting and Theatre Sociology at the University of Ibadan, Nigeria.

d'Abdon, Raphael is the author of three poetry collections, *sunnyside nightwalk* (2013), *salt water* (2016) and *the bitter herb* (2018), and the editor of the volumes I *nostri semi/Peo tsa rona. Poeti sudafricani del post-apartheid* (2007) and *Marikana: A Moment in Time* (2013). His poems have appeared in journals, magazines and anthologies in South Africa, Nigeria, Ghana, Malawi, Singapore, Palestine, India, Italy, USA and UK. He has read his poetry in South Africa, Nigeria, Somaliland, Italy and the USA, and is South Africa's representative of the AHN (Africa Haiku Network).

Disele, Lebogang is a doctoral student at the University of Alberta and a lecturer at the University of Botswana. Disele is a performer-researcher, specializing in multidisciplinary work that focuses on issues of marginalisation, discrimination, prejudice, and oppression, especially in relation to gender. Recent performance and production credits include *Words Unzipped*, *The Thread that Binds*, *Unwoven*, *What (Black) Life Requires*.

Edaki, Timothy. O is a final year undergraduate student of Mass Communication at the University of Benin. His works have appeared in *Kalahari Review, Praxis Magazine Online, EverGreen Poetry Journal, Sub-Saharan Magazine, Tush Magazine* and elsewhere. Timothy was a top entrant for the 2018 Lagos State International Poetry Festival.

Ede, Amatoritsero is a Nigerian-Canadian Africanist scholar, poet, and publisher of *Maple Tree Literary Supplement* (MTLS). His first book, *A Writer's Pains* (1998), won the 1998 ANA/Christopher Okigbo Prize for Poetry, and his second, *Globetrotter* (2009), was nominated for the 2013 The Nigeria Prize for Literature. He is an Assistant Professor of English at the University of The Bahamas.

Ekundayo, Omowumi Olabode Steven is a public speaker and writer based in Benin City, Nigeria. He holds a Ph.D. in English and Literature from the Department of English and Literature, University of Benin where he teaches grammar courses and writing. Ekundayo works include *Smile of a Goat, Queen Liegeria, Their Mistress,* and *Death, Be You Proud*.

Ekweremadu, Uchenna-Franklin's poetry manuscript, *Living on as Dust*, was shortlisted for the 2017 RL Poetry Award. His works have appeared in *Jalada Africa, Transition Magazine, Grub Street Journal, Saraba Magazine, Write Mag, Wilderness House Literary Review, Sentinel Nigeria Literary,* and *A&U American AIDS Magazine*. Ekweremadu lives in Kaduna, Nigeria.

Emetulu, Kennedy read History at the University of Benin, Nigeria and Law at the University of Lagos, Nigeria and at The College of Law, London, England. Emetulu is a public affairs consultant, social commentator, and a lover of literature.

Fabikun, Oyinkansade is the author of *Back to Basics: A guide to modern etiquette for students and young adults*. Fabikun is the founder of *Her Social Highness*, an institute whose vision is to promote civility through quality education in Nigeria.

Gatawa, Maryam studied Economics at Bayero University, Kano, Nigeria. Gatawa's works have appeared in *African Writer Magazine*,

Praxis Magazine, Ink Sweat and Tears, PIN Quarterly Magazine, Tuck Magazine, Better Than StarBucks, Anthology of Best New African Poets 2017, and *Kalahari Review.*

Gbolahan, Rasaq Malik is a graduate of the University of Ibadan. He is the author of the poetry chapbook, *No Home in This Land.* His poems have been published in *Sentinel, Saraba, African Writers, One, Rattle, Michigan Quaterly Review, Spillway, Poet Lore, Minnesota Review,* and elsewhere. Gbolahan is working on a memoir, and lives in Ibadan.

Gowk, Manasseh is a consultant and social activist based in Ghana. His work has been rewarded with an international poetry award in Italy, and a scholarship to attend the inaugural Migration Ethnicity Race and Health Congress, Edinburgh. He served as an education consultant with British Council, Ghana, and PFL Education International. Gowk's work has also received recognition from the YALI Network U.S., an initiative of President Barack Obama.

Habila, Helon is the author of four novels: *Waiting for an Angel, Measuring Time, Oil on Water*, and *Travelers,* and a nonfiction book, *The Chibok Girls.* He has co-edited the following works: *New Writing 14,* and *The Granta Book of the African Short Story.* He has won numerous awards including the Caine Prize for African Writing in 2001, Commonwealth Writers' Prize in 2002, and a Windham-Campbell prize for Fiction in 2015. Habila is professor of creative writing at George Mason University, U.S.A.

Hope, Akua Lezli is an African American artist and writer. She has won the US National Endowment of the Arts and the New York Foundation for the Arts fellowships for poetry. Her first collection, *Embouchure,* won a Writers' Digest Award. Her new collection, *Them Gone,* was published by The Word Works. Hope is a nominee for the 2019 Pushcart Prize.

Ibezim, Obinna Chukwudi teaches in the Department of English and Literary Studies, Alex Ekwueme Federal University, Ndufu-Alike Ikwo, Ebonyi State, Nigeria. Ibezim is a priest of the Church of Nigeria, Anglican Communion.

Ibukunoluwa, Janet James is a graduate of English language at Adeyemi college of Education, Ondo, Nigeria.

Ige, Ololade Akinlabi is an alumnus of Obafemi Awolowo University (OAU), Nigeria. He was a nominee for Nigerian Writers Award 2017, a two-time winner of Poets in Nigeria 10-day Poetry Challenge, and the second runner-up in Youth Shades international poetry contest in 2017. He was shortlisted for Albert Jungan poetry prize same year. Ige won the last edition of Ken Egba Poetry prize.

Ijalusi, Tola serves as a mentor in the Spring Literary Movements Mentorship Programme and the Managing Editor of *PAROUSIA Magazine*. A recipient of PIN Excellence Award 2016, Ijalusi has had his works published in *Muse for World Peace II & III, Peace is Possible, The Sun Will Rise Again, Writing Grandmothers Anthology,* and *Best New African Poets Anthology 2016 and 2017.*

Ijir, Martin earned a Bachelor of Education (Economics) from Anambra State University, Uli. He won the Lontano da casa won menzioni d'onore the Premio Internazionale di Letteratura e Fotografia Sentieri diVersi in 2019. Martin lives in Karu, Nasarawa State, Nigeria.

Imam, Khalid is a teacher, essayist, editor, translator, literary columnist, and author of twelve books, including, *The Song of San Kano, The Amigo Sisters,* and *Hirarrakin Bukar Usman*. He is Chairman of Arewa Teen Authors' Committee, Vice-Chairman of the Kano chapter of the Association of Nigerian Authors (ANA); a member of the Board of Trustee for Poets in Nigeria, and Executive Director of Whetstone Arts and Translation Services.

Inya, Richard works at Alex Ekwueme Federal University Ndufu-Alike Ikwo, Ebonyi State. He is the Chairman, Association of Nigerian Authors (ANA) Ebonyi State Branch. His works have been adopted for use in over eight states in Nigeria.

Israel, Winlade is a multilingual Nigerian writer whose works are written in Yoruba, French and English. He graduated from Obafemi Awolowo University, Ile-Ife in 2019 and teaches French at Destiny International College, Oshogbo. His poem, "Before Dusk," was rated among the top 100 poems submitted for Nigerian Students Poetry Prize in 2018.

James, Not'in (Richard Kayode O. James) self-identifies as an experimental artist & poet exploring the body, innings of power, instability and class in relation to the universality of individual experiences. His works often explore the trajectory of existing as one and in wholes.

Karounwi, Tenibegi (Samsideen Adesiyan) studied Theatre Arts at the University of Ibadan. He is rounding off a Law degree at Lead City University, Ibadan. Karounwi has had his poems published by the

Society of Young Nigerian Writers, and has had his plays performed in the Jos International Theatre Festival and at the Osun Osogbo Festival.

Katz-Lavigne, Sarah is completing a PhD dissertation in International Relations for a joint degree at Carleton University and the University of Groningen in the Netherlands. Her research focuses on conflict at and around large-scale mine sites in the Democratic Republic of Congo. Katz-Lavigne is an advocate for various causes including visa refusals to African scholars.

Keteku, Ian was crowned World Slam Poetry champion in France in the summer of 2010. Poet and multimedia artist, he was raised by Ghanaian parents and his work is influenced by his upbringing and journeys throughout Africa and Canada. His work follows in the lineage of ancient African storytellers by paying homage to the past and revisiting themes and lessons from previous generations. Keteku, who defines his poetry as "critical oratory," lives in Canada.

Kilanko, Yejide is a novelist and short fiction writer. Her debut novel, *Daughters Who Walk This Path (2012)*, a Canadian national bestseller, was longlisted for the inaugural Etisalat Prize and The Nigeria Prize for Literature. Her works includes a novella, *Chasing Butterflies* and a children's picture book, *There Is an Elephant in My Wardrobe*. Her short fiction is included in the anthology, *New Orleans Review* 2017: *The African Literary Hustle*. Kilanko lives in Ontario, Canada, where she also practices as a therapist in children's mental health.

King, Nseabasi S. J. is a media consultant, newspaper columnist, and former Head of Media, Office of the Deputy Governor of Akwa Ibom State, Nigeria. In 2018, he joined the Red Card Movement alongside former presidential candidate and political activisit, Dr. Oby Ezekwesili, as its Program Lead, Office of the Citizen, to speak against complacency in the Nigerian state. King lives in Calabar, Nigeria.

Macheso, Wesley is a Malawian studying for a PhD in Literature at Stellenbosch University, South Africa. He teaches literature at the University of Malawi. His short story "This Land is Mine" was published in *Water: new short story fiction from Africa* by Short Story Day Africa. Macheso won the 2014/ 2015 Peer Gynt Literary Award in Malawi for his children's book *Akuzike and the Gods*.

Madueke, Kingsley L. holds a PhD in Political Science from the University of Amsterdam, Netherlands. Madueke was a Marie

Skłodowska-Curie scholar from September 2014 – August 2015 and the winner of the David and Helen Kimble Prize for best academic article in 2018.

Mainza, Ludwidzi M. K. is a self-taught Zambian writer. His love of poetry started in secondary school where his very first poem earned him an award. He has been featured on Poetry Lounge, a local radio program showcasing emerging poets. He is an accountant by day and a writer at night. He is working on his first collection of poetry and prose book. Mainza lives in Lusaka, Zambia.

Makokha, Justus K. S. is a Kenyan poet, critic, translator, and academic. He teaches in the Department of Literature, Linguistics and Foreign Languages, Kenyatta University, Kenya. He is a member of the Advisory Board of the Institute of African Studies, Kenyatta University, Kenya. Makokha was a mentee of the late Prof. Pius Adesanmi.

Martins, Ndubuisi (Aniemeka) teaches Use of English and Writing at the Centre for General Studies, University of Ibadan. He has also taught Creative Writing, Literary Theory, Caribbean, African and African American literatures as an adjunct lecturer at McPherson University, Seriki Sotayo, Ogun State, Nigeria. Martins's poems have appeared in *Lines from the Rock*, *African writer*, and *Ngiga Review*.

Masinga, Nkateko is a South African poet and 2019 Fellow of the Ebedi International Writers Residency. She was nominated for a Pushcart Prize in 2018 and her work has received support from Pro Helvetia Johannesburg and the Swiss Arts Council. Masinga is the Contributing Interviewer for Poetry at *Africa in Dialogue*, an online interview magazine.

Midgley, Peter is an editor, playwright, storyteller, and children's novelist. He has performed in several countries around the world. His works include: *Thuli's Mattress*, *perhaps I should/miskien moet ek*, and *Unquiet Bones*. His latest poetry collection is *let us not think of them as barbarians*.

Mofehintoluwa, Koye-Ladele is a Law student at Obafemi Awolowo University, Ile-Ife, Nigeria. Besides creative writing, Mofehintoluwa writes Op-ed articles for *Sahara Reporters*, *Premium Times* (Campus Reporter), *Nairaland* and other online newspapers.

Nduka, Echezonachukwu is the author of *Chrysanthemums for Wide-eyed Ghosts*. The recipient of the 2016 Korea-Nigeria Poetry Feast Prize, his works have appeared in *Transition*, *River River*, *Bombay*

Review, Maple Tree Literary Supplement, Saraba, Jalada Africa, Brittle Paper, among others. Nduka is a member of South Jersey Poets Collective and lives in New Jersey, where he teaches music and performs as a pianist.

Nduka, Uche is the prolific author of about a dozen books of poetry and prose, including *Living in Public, Nine East, Ijele, eel on reef, Heart's Field, If Only the Night,* and *Chiaroscuro,* which won the Association of Nigerian Authors Poetry Prize in 1997. Nduka, also an essayist and photographer who lives in Brooklyn, U.S., holds a Bachelor of Arts degree from the University of Nigeria and a Master of Fine Arts from Long Island University.

Nebeolisa, Okwudili won the inaugural Jalada Prize in poetry. His works have appeared in *The Threepenny Review, The Cincinnati Review, Fireside Fiction, Commonwealth Writers, Catapult, Salamander Magazine,* and others. Nebeolisa's works have been recognized as finalist or shortlisted for the Gerald Kraak Award, the Sillerman Prize for African Poet, the Tom Howard/John H Reid Fiction & Essay Contest, and the Raedleaf Poetry Competition in the international category.

Nnaji, James Onyebụchi is a graduate of English at the University of Nigeria, Nsukka, where he edited *The Muse: A Journal of English and Literary Studies*, no. 39. His writing has appeared in *The Muse, Drumtide Magazine, The Nasiona Magazine* and *Ogele*. In 2011, Nnaji won the poetry prize at the University of Nigeria Literary Art Festival and the Emeka Anuforo/University of Nigeria Prize for Literary Artist of the Year.

Noah, Nathanael Tanko holds a Master of Arts Education (English Language Education) degree from the University of Jos, Nigeria. He is the author of *A Dance of Stanzas, Frontispieces, Black Woman of Africa*, and *My Book of Nursery Rhymes*. Noah lives in Jos, Nigeria.

Ntuli, Sihle a South African, is a former Classical Mythology lecturer and recipient of a 2019 Innovation Award. His poems have been published in *New Coin, Jalada, Bakwa* and *Saraba*, amongst others. Ntuli has also been published in anthologies such as the *Best New African Poets 2015 Anthology* and the *Sol Plaatjie European Union Poetry Anthology* Vol VIII.

Nwadike, Ifesinachi holds a Master of Arts degree in Literature from the University of Ibadan, respectively. A 2018 Ebedi International

Writers Residency Fellow, Nwadike is the Founding Editor of *Ngiga Review*. Nwadike lives in Ibadan.

Nwafor, Ugochukwu P., is a lawyer whose work has appeared in *Lunaris Review, Fox Spirit Book, Active Muse*, and *Enkare Review*. He bagged his LL. B from the Nnamdi Azikiwe University, and his B.L from the Nigerian Law School, Abuja. Nwafor shares his time between the U.S. and Nigeria.

Nwizu, Gloria is a Nigerian-American finishing an Associate degree in criminology at Gwinnett Technical College in Georgia and is slated to begin her studies for a BA in Comparative Literature by spring of 2020. She is polishing a poetry collection due for publication in 2020. An essayist and an opera vocalist in training, Gloria lives in metro Atlanta, U.S.

Nwokolo, Chuma, a law graduate of the University of Nigeria, was called to the Nigerian bar in 1984. His novels include *Diaries of a Dead African, One More Tale for the Road,* and *The Extinction of Menai*. Some of his short stories are collected in *The Ghost of Sani Abacha, How to Spell Naija in 100 Short Stories Volume 1* and *How to Spell Naija in 100 Short Stories Volume 2*. His poetry collections include *Memories of Stone* and *The Final Testament of a Minor God*. Nwokolo is the convener of the Bribecode good governance campaign.

Nwulia, Augustine Ogechukwu is a conference/motivational speaker and public-speaking coach. A research fellow and columnist for numerous pan-African newspapers, Nwulia is the founder of The Black Diary, an advocacy project invested in restoring hope and igniting the spirit of determination in society.

Obemata is the pseudonym of Abdul Mahmud, an Abuja, Nigeria-based lawyer and author of *Triptych* (poems). Obemata's latest collection of poems, *Three Sections: Extracts from the Address to the Alter Ego* and *Book of Soliloquies*, and a collection of essays, *Caution: Demolition Work in Progress – Thoughts on a Ruin Nation*, are in press.

Obiwu teaches English in the Department of Humanities, Central State University, Ohio, United States. His poetry volumes include *Tigress at Full Moon* and *Rituals of the Sun*. He was a fellow of the Presidential Leadership Institute, Central State University, Wilberforce, Ohio, and a fellow of the International School of Theory in the Humanities. Obiwu is co-editor of *The Critical Imagination in African Literature: Essays in Honor of Michael J.C. Echeruo*.

Odonwodo, Uzo was born in Bamenda, Cameroon. He holds an LLB from the University of Nigeria and an LLM from Michigan State University. He is licensed to practice law in Nigeria and in the state of New York in the Unites States. The former editor of the *Nwa Okike* journal at the University of Nigeria, Enugu Campus, his poems and short stories have been published widely. Odonwodo is an investor and amateur photographer.

Ogbedeto, Chimeziri C. is a lecturer at the Federal Polytechnic, Nekede, Nigeria, where she teaches English Language and Literature-in-English. Ogbedeto is studying for a doctoral degree in African Literature at Imo State University, Owerri.

Ogbogu, Ubaka is an award-winning legal scholar and poet. He is an associate professor in the Faculties of Law and Pharmacy/Pharmaceutical Studies, and the Katz Research Fellow in Health Law and Policy, at the University of Alberta, Canada, and the author of the collection of poems, *Bread and Blood Tonics* (2005). His work-in-progress, *Nostalgia, is* a new collection of poems in which he re-imagines his childhood as a conflict between light and darkness, truth and lies, and concord and dissonance.

Ogundayo, 'BioDun J. is an associate professor of French and Comparative Literature at the Bradford campus of the University of Pittsburgh, USA, where he is the director of the Africana Studies program. Ogundayo is a co-editor of *African Sacred Spaces* published by Lexington Books, U.S.A.

Ogungbe, 'Bunmi is an early-career Epidemiologist, whose primary research interest is in cardiovascular diseases among immigrant population. When she is not scratching her head about another error message on the SAS program, Ogungbe can be found writing and reading.

Ogunleye, Moses studied Typology of Pottery, Artifacts and Monolithic Findings in the Archaeology and Anthropology Department of the University of Ibadan, Nigeria, where he also served as a Senior Art Assistant before joining VSA Arts of Nigeria as a board member in 2012. Ogunleye's commissioned works include "Dance Africa," a wall mural commissioned by Brooklyn Center for Arts and Culture and "Portraits of Nelson Mandela," commissioned by Professor Toyin

Falola for the book *Mandela: Tributes to a Global Icon*. Ogunleye lives in New York City.

Ohiemi, Anthony Enyone graduated with a Bachelor of Arts in English Literature from Ahmadu Bello University, Zaria, Nigeria, and a Master's in English Literature from Bayero University, Kano. His poems have appeared in *The Lectern* and *Gombe Copa*. Ohiemi is a Customer Care Analyst in the Telecommunications industry in Kano, Nigeria.

Okeigwe, Sunny Iyke U. holds a B.A. degree in English and Literary Studies from Imo State University, Owerri, Nigeria. Okeigwe has taught English Language and Literature at UNIBEK College, Graceland International School, and other schools in Port Harcourt, Nigeria.

Okeke, Ethel Ngozi recently defended her PhD thesis entitled "Sex and Sexuality in Selected Works of Contemporary Nigerian Novelists" at the Department of Linguistics and Literary Studies of Ebonyi State University. Okeke lectures at the General Studies Division, Enugu State University of Science.

Okorie, Mitterand is a doctoral student in Conflict Transformation and Peace Studies at the University of KwaZulu-Natal, Durban, South Africa. He holds a Bachelor of Arts and Master's in science from *Eastern Mediterranean* University, Cyprus and Aberystwyth University, United Kingdom. Okorie is author of the novel, *All That Was Bright and Ugly*.

Olabode, Segun Michael earned a Bachelor of Arts in Theatre Arts from the University of Ibadan, Nigeria. A stage director and drama teacher, his poems have appeared in *Praxis magazine,* and *Kalahari Review*. Olabode lives in Lagos, Nigeria.

Olaniyan, Olumide published his debut poetry collection *Lucidity of Absurdity* in 2017. Olaniyan's poem, "Behind Closed Doors," won the maiden edition of Communicators' League Creative Writing Contest in 2017. Another poem, "Deja vu," has been adapted into a play. "One Sojourn of the Moon" received an honorary mention in the Mandela Day Poetry Competition 2016.

Olapegba, Peter Olamakinde is professor of Social Psychology at the University of Ibadan, Nigeria. Besides teaching and research into psychological phenomena, Olapegba enjoys traveling and reading literature.

Oloyede, Kafilat holds a Master of Arts in Communication and Language Arts from the University of Ibadan. She has taught for over 14 years before joining development work. Oloyede was an English Language and Literature in English Teacher in several secondary schools in Oyo State after which she taught Use of English and Communication in English for ten years at the Polytechnic, Ibadan.

Onoruoiza, Onuchi Mark is a corporate communications and high-impact business re-engineering consultant at a consulting group. Onoruoiza is a Certified Negotiation Specialist from the Transatlantic School of Business and also an Innovation Catalyst from the Global Innovation Management Institute.

Osuji, Clara Ijeoma holds a Ph.D. in English from the University of Lagos, Nigeria, where she also serves as a Graduate Research Fellow. Her research interest includes men and masculinities with a focus on fatherhood. Osuji's ongoing scholarly projects encompass aging masculinities, father-son relationships, and female fatherhood.

Osundare, Niyi is a Distinguished Professor of English, University of New Orleans. He is the prolific author of over 18 books of poetry, four plays, a book of essays and some monographs. One of Africa's most decorated poets, Osundare's awards include the Nigerian National Merit Award; Fellow of the Nigeria Academy of Letters; the Tchicaya U Tam'si Award for African poetry; the Fonlon/Nichols Award; the Commonwealth Poetry Prize, and the NOMA award for publishing in Africa.

Otieno, Sam Dennis is a PhD candidate in Literature at the University of Nairobi. His research work focuses on visual arts as a means of self-narration in East Africa. He teaches West African Literature at the University of Nairobi.

Otiono, Nduka is a professor of African Studies and Graduate Program Coordinator at the Institute of African Studies, Carleton University, Ottawa, Canada. Along with two volumes of poetry (*Voices in the Rainbow* and *Love in a Time of Nightmares*), and a collection of short stories (*The Night Hides with a Knife*), he is co-editor of *We-Men: An Anthology of Men Writing on Women* and *Camouflage: Best of Contemporary Writing from Nigeria*. His co-edited volume of scholarly essays, *Polyvocal Bob Dylan: Music, Performance, Literature,* was recently published by Palgrave Macmillan. Otiono has won prizes for his books of fiction and poetry, as well as for excellence in teaching, research, and community building.

Ramakrishna, Anushya is a student at the National Law School of India University. Although she came from an impoverished family, she was given a very good education from Shanti Bhavan. Her vision is to build a school like Shanti Bhavan that provided her a world-class education for hundred more children like herself. Ramakrishna enjoys writing poetry.

Salawu, Olajide is the author of *Preface for Leaving Homeland* published under African Poetry Book Fund chapbook box set series. He was a 2017 Pushcart Prize nominee. His poems have appeared in *Transition, New Orleans Review, Prosopisia, Paragrammer, Wacammaw*, among others. Salawu has a Master's in Literary Studies from the Department of English, Obafemi Awolowo University in Ile-Ife, Nigeria, where he lives.

Salawudeen, Saudat is a student of computer science and an art aficionado. Salawudeen lives and works in Nigeria.

Senaratne, Uthpala Dishani is a poet and short story writer. She obtained her Bachelor's degree in English from the University of Peradeniya, Sri Lanka, and her Master's in Linguistics at the University of Kelaniya, Sri Lanka. Senaratne has been an instructor in English in Sri Lanka.

Shehu, Emman Usman is the author of three poetry collections: *Questions for Big Brother, Open Sesame* and *Icarus Rising*. He works in Abuja where he heads the International Institute of Journalism. Shehu's literary activism includes running a writers' outfit, undertaking creative writing workshops and editing the literary journal *Dugwe*.

Sibanda, Ndaba has compiled and edited *Its Time*, and *Free Fall*. He is the author of *Love O'clock, The Dead Must Be Sobbing, Football of Fools, Of the Saliva and the Tongue* and *When Inspiration Sings in Silence*. Sibanda hails from Bulawayo, Zimbabwe.

Smith, Pamela J. Olúbùnmi is a retired professor of English, Humanities and Women's Studies in the Goodrich Scholarship Program at the University of Nebraska at Oma. She taught English Composition, Women & Gender Studies ("Women of Color Writers") and Humanities courses for over three decades. Her research interests and publications are in the areas of translation studies and

Yorùbá Language and Literature. Smith has won numerous grant awards for research and teaching, among them UNO's prestigious Excellence in Teaching Award.

Taiwo, Yusuf Taslemat is a student of Law at the University of Lagos, Nigeria. Taiwo is a spoken words artiste and blogger.

Tsaaior, James Tar is Professor of Media and Cultural Communication at Pan-Atlantic University, Lagos. He has published two volumes of poetry: *Moments and Monuments* and *I Am Chibok*. The Director, Academic Planning of the University and editor, *Journal of Cultural and Media Studies of* Pan-Atlantic University, Lagos, he is an Alexander von Humboldt Experienced Researcher in Berlin and the University of Potsdam, Germany. Tsaaior was also a Leverhulme Trust and Isaac Newton Visiting Research Fellow, University of Cambridge, U.K.

Túbọsún, Kọlá is a Lagos-based writer and linguist. A 2016 recipient of the Premio Ostana Prize for writings in the mother tongue, Túbọsún, a Miles Morland Writing Scholar, is the author of *Edwardsville by Heart*.

Ugwu, Ejiofor lives in New York where he is a Master of Fine Arts student of poetry at Syracuse University. He was among the 2017 Ten New Generation African Poets organized by African Poetry Book Fund and edited by Kwame Dawes and Chris Abani, where his chapbook, *The Book of God* was published. Ugwu's writing has also been published in *Guernica*, *African American Review*, *Public Pool*, *The Poetry Society* (UK), *Poetry Society of America*, and the University of Nigeria's journal, *The Muse*, for which he edited poetry for its 40th edition in 2012.

Umezurike, Uchechukwu is a doctoral candidate and Vanier Scholar at the Department of English and Film Studies, University of Alberta, Edmonton, Canada. An Alumnus of the Iowa International Writing Program, has participated in residencies in Ghana, India, Switzerland and Italy. He has twice been shortlisted for The Nigeria Prize for Literature (2007 and 2011), and was one of the winners of the Commonwealth Short Story Competition in 2006 and 2008. Umezurike is the author of the children's books, *Gogo and the Slimy Green Grub* and *The Boy who Throw Stones at Animals and Other Stories* as well as many other creative works published in several anthologies.

Uzoatu, Uzor Maxim is a Nigerian writer and journalist who began his career as a rural peasant theatre director of plays. He was a Distinguished Visitor at the Graduate School of Journalism, University of Western Ontario, Canada, and a nominee for the Caine Prize for African Writing in 2008. He has published three novels: *Satan's Story*, *Day of Blood and Fire*, and *The Missing Link*; two plays: *A Play of Ghosts* and *Doctor of Football*; and a collection of poems *God of Poetry*. Also, the author of a human rights book, *The Way We Are*, Uzoatu has recently completed a new creative non-fiction book, *How Not to be a Nigerian*.

Verissimo, Jumoke is a doctoral student in the Department of English and Film Studies, University of Alberta, Canada. The author of two collections of poetry (*I am Memory* and *The Birth of Illusion)*, she has also published a chapbook with *Saraba Magazine,* titled *Epiphanies*. Her poetry has been translated into French, Chinese, Japanese, Macedonian, and Norwegian. *A Small Silence (*2019) *is* her debut novel from Cassava Republic Press.

Vincent, John Chizoba is a Lagos-based poet, cinematographer and filmmaker. His works have appeared in *Africanwriter, Tuck Magazine*, *Gaze, Praxis magazine*, and elsewhere. Vincent is the author of *Good Mama, Hard times, Letter from Home,* and *For Boys of Tomorrow*.

Waweru, Margaret Wairimu holds a Bachelor of Education degree from Masinde Muliro University of Science and Technology in Kenya. She is pursuing a Master's in English Literature in Mount Kenya University. Some of her poems have appeared in *Arthut*, *The campus magazine*, *World of dreams poetry* and *The Hopewell*. Waweru lives in Nairobi, Kenya.

Whyte, Daniel Olaoluwa is a final year student of English and literary studies at the Federal University, Oye-Ekiti, Ekiti State, Nigeria. Whyte was the first runner-up of Gbemisola Adeoti Poetry Competition (2018) with his poem "Who is Lakunle Alara?" He is also a campus journalist whose writing has appeared in *African Progressive Economist* and *The Cable*, among others. Whyte lives in Ibadan, Nigeria.

Yeku, James is a professor of African digital humanities at The University of Kansas. His article "Akpos Don Come Again: Nigerian Cyberpop Hero as Trickster" won the 2017 Best Article Award of the

African Literature Association. He is a member of the editorial board of the *Journal of African Cultural Studies*.

Yusuff, Abdulbasit studied Science Laboratory Technology at the Federal Polytechnic, Bida. Some of Abdulbasit's works have appeared in *Tuck Magazine* and *Spark of Hope: an anthology of poems for saving lives*.

Zulu, Chifwanti earned his Bachelor of Arts from the University of Zambia. He is the author of *A Penny for Your Thoughts*, a WordPress personal blog of poetry and daily musings. Zulu works as a call quality-monitoring representative in Lusaka, Zambia.

About the editors

Nduka Otiono is a writer, Assistant Professor and Graduate Program Coordinator at the Institute of African Studies, Carleton University. Prior to turning to academia, he was for many years a journalist in Nigeria. His works have appeared in *Journal of Folklore Research*, *African Literature Today*, *Journal of African Cinema*, *Transfers: Interdisciplinary Journal of Mobility Studies*, *Wasafiri*, etc. His co-edited volume of essays, *Polyvocal Bob Dylan: Music, Performance, Literature* was recently published under the imprint of Palgrave Macmillan Studies in Music and Literature Series. Otiono is winner of a Capital Educator's Award for Excellence in Teaching, a Carleton University Faculty of Arts and Social Sciences Early Career Award for Research Excellence, twice winner of the Carnegie Africa Diaspora Fellowship, and a 2018 Black History Ottawa Community Builder Award. He is the author of *The Night Hides with a Knife* (short stories), which won the ANA/Spectrum Prize; *Voices in the Rainbow* (Poetry), a finalist for the ANA/Cadbury Poetry Prize; *Love in a Time of Nightmares* (Poetry) for which he was awarded the James Patrick Folinsbee Memorial Scholarship in Creative Writing. He has co-edited *We-Men: An Anthology of Men Writing on Women* (1998), and *Camouflage: Best of Contemporary Writing from Nigeria* (2006).

Uchechukwu Umezurike is a PhD Candidate and Vanier Scholar in the English and Film Studies department of the University of Alberta, Canada. An Alumnus of the International Writing Program (USA), he has participated in residencies in India, Switzerland, and Italy. His poem "there's more" won the 2019 *National Norma Epstein Foundation Award for Creative Writing*. He was one of the winners of the *Commonwealth Short Story Competition* in 2006 and 2008. His children's books *Sam and the Wallet* and *The Runaway Hero* have been shortlisted and longlisted for the *Nigeria Prize for Literature* in 2007 and 2011 respectively. His creative writing has appeared in the following publications: *The Lamp, Evergreen Review, Onomonresoa, On Broken Wings, Long Story Short, Dream Chasers, Migrations, Lagos of the Poets, Washington Square Review, African Roar, Daughters of*

Eve and Other Stories. His critical writing has appeared in *Tydskrif vir Letterkunde, Postcolonial Text, Journal of African Cultural Studies, Cultural Studies, Journal of African Literature Association,* and *African Literature Today.*

CPSIA information can be obtained
at www.ICGtesting.com
Printed in the USA
LVHW010357030320
648723LV00004B/882